T0159651

Secrets to Successful
Property Investment

Secrets to Successful Property Investment

Deborah Durbin

BUSINESS
BOOKS

Winchester, UK
Washington, USA

JOHN HUNT PUBLISHING

First published by Business Books, 2021
Business Books is an imprint of John Hunt Publishing Ltd., No. 3 East St., Alresford,
Hampshire SO24 9EE, UK
office@jhpbooks.com
www.johnhuntpublishing.com
www.johnhuntpublishing.com/business-books

For distributor details and how to order please visit the 'Ordering' section on our website.

Text copyright: Deborah Durbin 2020

ISBN: 978 1 78904 818 6
978 1 78904 819 3 (ebook)
Library of Congress Control Number: 2020949048

A CIP catalogue record for this book is available from the British Library.

Design: Stuart Davies

Printed and bound by TJ Books Limited, Padstow, Cornwall

We operate a distinctive and ethical publishing philosophy in
all areas of our business, from our global network of authors to
production and worldwide distribution.

Contents

This book is dedicated to
the risk takers of the world

About the Authors

Deborah Durbin

Deborah began investing in property in 2013 when she bought her first property – a rundown three-bed house at an auction, using all her savings. After renovating it, she sold it for a profit and used that money as a deposit on a buy-to-let property.

Since then, Deborah has bought over 30 rental properties and has built her portfolio by leveraging the capital from early purchases to finance additional properties.

Deborah's motto has always been; *If you don't ask, you won't get*, and this has stood the test of time in her career as a property developer and investor and continues to do so. She's a firm believer in taking calculated risks because without them, you will always remain where you are.

Having been a journalist, columnist, and bestselling author for most of her adult life, she decided it was about time to put pen to paper and share her knowledge and secrets about how to succeed at property investment.

Jason Whitehead

From leaving college and a summer job as a builder, Jason took his first real career steps into finance with Cheltenham and Gloucester Building Society.

Little did he know just where this path would lead to. Whilst there he was involved with the home mortgage advisor scheme.

In 2013 Jason started his own mortgage company, Vitality Mortgages Ltd and has worked with Deborah ever since she called him up and asked for his advice.

*All the information in this book is correct at the time of writing.

Acknowledgements

I literally knew nothing about property investment when I started my property business seven years ago. As a child, I grew up in a council house and as an adult, I always rented my homes, so I had zero experience of dealing with estate agents and solicitors, let alone persuading a mortgage company to lend me hundreds of thousands of pounds to buy a property. And to be honest, this was never part of my 'life plan'.

I always say I'm a reluctant property investor/landlord because owning property just wasn't something I had ever been taught and being a freelance journalist and writer, my income was always so sporadic that I felt renting was really the only option for me.

It was only when I was talking to a friend who worked in finance about whether I should put the little savings I had into a private pension, and he suggested I buy a property instead, did I even consider this could be an option.

Seven years later I have a property portfolio worth millions of pounds and an income which means I'm not tied to a 9-5 job and I have the freedom to work when I want, whilst still having financial security.

Whist there are many deserving books/podcasts/videos out there on how to get started in buying property, this book details what I have personally learned over the years. No two property investors do it the same way. Some are happy with managing one or two properties, others specialise in luxury apartments or commercial property, but the basic investment strategies are the same – buy below market value, improve the property, and rent it out or sell it for a profit.

I've covered as many different property investment options as I can, but primarily this book is about how to start with buying your first property, what it will entail and how to expand your business.

There have been so many people who have helped me in my journey and who have taught me so much. From my financial advisor and mortgage brokers, Jason and Natalie Whitehead who have the patience of a saint as they repeatedly explain to me for the hundredth time about mortgage options and interest rates. Jason has also very kindly provided the financial information for this book.

My thanks go out to my accountant, Heather who tirelessly keeps my accounts up to date and often points out that not every meal out can be claimed as a business meeting expense.

Thank you to Dan, who sold me one of my first properties and has been one of my best friends ever since and who still continues to advise me of what property is a good investment.

Thanks to my lettings team at Westcoast Properties who have been my letting agents since day one and have always had my best interests at heart. And to Weston Support Services (particularly Matt and Becky) who make sure all my property maintenance is taken care of.

A big thank you to the National Residential Landlord Association (NRLA) for all their help and advice, particularly when I had to take a tenant to court for the first time. The people at PIMS (Property Information Made Simple) for all their tenancy advice and Mike at my local CAB who helped me when I had to start legal proceedings against a cowboy builder.

I would also like to thank those people who turned out to be less than genuine and honest; all you did was made me a stronger person. Finally, thank you to my publishers who believed in me and the need for this book.

Introduction

Whilst there is always a risk with any investment, property is widely considered to be one of the safest forms of investment. Regardless of whether we experience another recession, property will continue to be one of the most profitable investment options, and the reason for this is that people will always need somewhere to live.

Over the years the UK government have made it increasingly difficult for people to own their own home. With the withdrawal of 100% deposit mortgages in 2007/08, it meant that only people who had saved enough money for a deposit could get on the property ladder.

Although there are now a few lenders who still offer a 0% mortgage, the conditions are that the deposit is secured by a guarantor such as a parent, who is willing to secure their own home or assets against the loan.

At the time of writing, there is talk of offering 95% mortgages to enable first-time buyers to get a step on the property ladder, but this has yet to be decided and I do wonder what the interest rates are going to be if this comes into effect.

Consequently, it is increasingly difficult for anyone to buy their own home and as such, most have no option but to rent.

Added to this, due to the decrease in available social housing properties available in the UK, many people have to rent privately from the private rental sector. According to a recent Gov.UK study, 5.8 million households will be privately rented by 2021. That's nearly one in every four households.

Whilst these figures are depressing to read and the fact that the majority of households renting don't think they will ever be able to afford to buy their own home, it does highlight the necessity for private rental properties, because the government still won't accept that we have a huge housing crisis on our hands.

If you have the tenacity and the money to invest in properties for the rental market, you could be sitting on a gold mine. Whether you buy a single property or create a portfolio of rental properties, with the help of this book you could reap the rewards by investing in the rental market.

This book is written by journalist and property expert, Deborah Durbin with financial input from financial advisor, Jason Whitehead of Vitality Mortgages Ltd. Whilst there are many other worthy titles about property investment out there, this draws on Deborah's personal experience, going from someone who knew nothing about property to becoming a multimillionaire investor in seven years.

As a female property investor, it can still be a challenge to be taken seriously within some mainly male-dominated industries such as finance, estate agencies and in the construction trade.

This book is that helping hand you need when you feel a bit overwhelmed by the process of property investment, enabling you to create a passive income and possibly never have to worry about money again.

Chapter One

Why Invest in Property?

Despite the UK Government's continuous attempts to make it difficult for people to invest in property (increased Stamp Duty, decreased tax exemptions, threats of another economic recession, to name a few), bricks and mortar are, in our opinion, still the best place to put your money. Pensions, Isa's, Stocks and Shares are and always have been a huge gamble.

Although there are still risks when putting your money into property, when done correctly, the benefits far outweigh the risks, and this is why...

Property is a basic necessity. Even if another recession hits – people will always need somewhere to live.

- A property is a tangible asset. Unlike other investments, it's a solid thing.
- Even though the property market will always go up and down, property investment is one of the safer forms of investment.
- There will always be a need for properties regardless of size.
- Property can give you one of the greatest returns in terms of investment.
- Investing in the rental market is a long-term investment option that will bring in a continual passive income.

Let's look at these points in more detail...

Property is a Basic Necessity:

At the time of writing this book, there is a huge shortage of rental properties in the UK. This is partly due to the fact that there are not enough social housing properties available to meet the number of people needing an affordable home. Secondly, mortgage lenders' criteria for lending money to buy a property are much more stringent than they used to be.

Then there is the issue of finding the deposit required to put down on a property. A recent study by the Halifax found that 88% of working families could not afford a deposit on a house. Consequently, the rental market has rocketed.

This means that if you are in the position to buy a second property as a buy-to-let, you will always be able to rent it out to tenants in need of a home.

Property is a Tangible Asset:

When you invest in a property, you are investing in something that is solid and real. It doesn't matter whether it's an apartment, a house, a HMO, or an entire block of flats. Property is a tangible asset and as such means you can do so much more than re-sell or rent it. Once you have an investment property, it is easy to use that asset to your advantage. As your property increases in value, you are able to pull money out of it to either reinvest in another property, or use it for other purposes, such as upgrading your car, taking a holiday, etc.

Property is One of the Safer Investments:

Whilst we are obliged to inform you that any investment of your hard-earned cash has its risks, investing in property is still one of the safest of investments. Done correctly it can generate an ongoing passive income for you; potentially earning you money while you sleep.

In the long-term as a property price increases, it makes a capital gain, which you can benefit from by reinvesting.

Obviously with any investment, there comes risk and property investment is no different. The way the UK Government look at taxation on rental properties can and often does change quickly.

You can also suffer from tenants refusing to pay their rent (we will look at this in depth later in the book) and you could be faced with rental void periods when a tenant vacates, and you have to find another tenant.

There Will Always be a Need for Property:

As mentioned in the first point, it doesn't matter who you are; unless you are happy living in a tent, you need somewhere to live. Because it is difficult for people to own their own property, the market for buying a property as a rental is huge at the moment, and the forecast suggests that this will increase, with the majority of homes being rented through the private sector.

In recent years, the government has enforced a lot of anti-landlord policies, including no longer being able to charge a prospective tenant for credit and reference checks and a cap on how much deposit a landlord can charge a tenant. Added to this there are less tax deductions that you can claim as a property investor.

However, as annoying as this is for any landlord, all it has done is encourage landlords to increase their rents to outweigh the extra costs and because over 80% of people rent their homes from landlords, there will never be a shortage of tenants for your property.

A Long-term Investment:

There is no investment option that is risk free and short-term. If you invest in stock and shares, Isa's or pensions, there is no guarantee that you will make or lose money. Investing in property is not a get-rich-quick option; it needs to be looked at as more of a long-term investment.

However, with property investment, in the short-term, if you rent a property, you will be generating a passive income from renting it out right from the start. In the long-term, your property will increase in value. This means that after 10 years, your property could have easily doubled in market value price (we'll discuss this in more detail later in the book).

Recessions will always come and go. Stats on the 2008 recession showed us that those landlords who braved it and held on to their properties during the '08 recession benefitted ten-fold from their investments. If you can weather the storm during an economic crisis, you will be one of the ones reaping the rewards when it all blows over.

Added to this, the more properties you add to your portfolio, the greater your passive income. To the point that you will no longer have to work in a job that you don't like and will have the financial freedom to live the life you choose.

Chapter Two

Where to Start?

A Little Food for Thought...

It's worth looking at some figures before we concentrate on where to start with property investment. For the majority of adults in the country, we are just one payday away from being in serious financial trouble.

It's a scary thought to think that if you lost your job tomorrow, many could only survive for a maximum of 30 days before they would be in debt. Given that we are living longer (the average age we live to is now 81), and the pension age has risen, means that if we have no other means of income, we have no choice but to work until we reach retirement age.

The current state pension is around (as of 2020) £170.00 per week. If you have had to take time off during your working life to raise children, care for a loved one, or due to illness or lack of jobs in your field, your state pension will be reduced. Yes, you can get top-ups in the form of pension credits to make up the shortfall, but this is the amount of money the government think that people can live off. That £170.00 has to cover all your living expenses; your rent/mortgage, your utility bills, your food etc, so there is very little, if anything, left over. This is your reward for working 40 hours a week for the past 45 years.

According to recent statistics, just 1% of people of retirement age are financially independent. 4% meet their basic needs. 22% have to continue working past retirement age to top up their pension. 28% rely totally on their state pension and 45% depend on family to help them out with their basic weekly needs.

It's shocking and worrying to see that almost half of people aged over 68 have to rely on others to just meet their daily living costs, and with us living longer, this figure will increase.

The 1% of people who are financially independent – and by this, I mean they don't have to work or rely on anyone else when they retire from work – are able to see their autumnal years in financial freedom. Most adults are so busy working to pay the bills, that they don't have the time or the money for a second or passive income. If you can invest in property as early as possible, you can increase your income to the point where you will no longer have to work in your job and you will never be reliant on the government or family to support you when you get older. In short, you will be financially independent, which means you will be able to do the things you want to do in life.

Residential and BTL Mortgages:

In the UK, you can only have one residential mortgage to your name. Depending on lenders' criteria, you can have many Buy-to-Let (BTL) mortgages. The main thing to consider when applying for a BTL mortgage is that your deposit will be significantly higher than that of a residential mortgage, but your repayments will be a lot less because the majority of BTL mortgages are interest only mortgages. A Buy-to-Let mortgage deposit is usually around 25% of the value of the property, whereas the deposit for most residential mortgages is between 5% and 15%, depending on the lender and the economic climate. Currently residential mortgage deposits are around 10% due to the higher economy risks due to Covid-19. Buy-to-Let deposits appear to have stayed at around 25%.

Sourcing a Deposit

Whenever I talk to anyone about investing in properties, they always say they would love to do it, but they have no idea where to start. In particular, they have no idea where they would get enough money for a deposit. If you don't have any savings, it can seem an impossible dream to get yourself on the property ladder, let alone think about investing in additional property to flip or rent.

However, there are many options out there that will help you find the money required for a deposit for a second property. Starting out can feel like you're at the bottom of a mountain, particularly if you have a low credit rating score, or you are already in debt, but it's not impossible.

You might not be in the position to start immediately, but it's worth making a plan now for the future where you will be seen as a good risk. This includes getting your credit history up to date and paying off any outstanding debts.

We urge anyone thinking about investing in property to find out what their current credit score is on the Experian website (www.experian.co.uk). This will give you a good idea of how lenders will see you as a good creditor. If your score is quite low, it will pay you to do as much as you can to increase it, by paying off any outstanding debts. It may be a slow process, but you will need to prove to lenders that you are a good risk if they are going to lend you money for a mortgage.

Where to find a deposit:

On most occasions, whenever you purchase a property, you will need to find the money for a deposit. On a property you wish to rent out (a Buy-to-Let, or BTL) it is usually 25% of the total price of the property. There are many options to generate your deposit and we have listed a few below:

Bank Loans:

As long as you have a good credit history banks are still willing to lend money and will often help with the deposit for a property. If, for example, the property costs £130,000, you are going to need £32,500 by way of a deposit, plus Stamp Duty if this is a second property (see the government's website for current rates), plus solicitor and valuation fees. You will be looking at needing to find around £37,000 to cover all your costs.

Banks will look at your ability to pay back the deposit loan. They will take into account your household take-home salary and any other regular money you have coming in. Bank loans can have high interest rates, so be aware of this when you are looking for this kind of finance.

Re-Mortgage:

If you already own your own home on a mortgage, you can contact your mortgage lender and ask them to re-mortgage your home, freeing up enough money for you to buy a second property. As long as you can afford the repayments and your property has increased in value, your mortgage lender will often oblige with a further advance. Most lenders will consider your income and ability to repay the mortgage should you be without a tenant for a period of time.

Credit Cards:

Not our favourite means of generating additional income, but I know that some property investors started out this way. Many credit card companies offer a 0% interest rate for a certain amount of time. I personally know of one investor who had four credit cards with £10,000 on each at 0% interest for two years. He used this to pay for the deposit on his first property. It's a bit of a risky way to do it, but after a quick redecoration, he sold the property, paid his credit cards and mortgage off, and still had enough left over to pay for the deposit on another property.

Friends and Family:

The bank of mum and dad is another option if you can't get a deposit together yourself. I've helped two of my daughters get their first buy-to-let properties by loaning them the deposit. You can ask friends or family if they could help out. Just make sure you have an agreement in writing, so that everyone knows where they stand.

Lenders:

There are some lenders who are more switched on than others and have seen that there is a shortage of affordable rental property on the market and are looking at different options to help new property investors. Due to the everchanging market, we can't stipulate which lenders are taking these new routes, but a good mortgage broker will have knowledge as to which lenders are moving with the times.

Joint Ventures:

A joint venture is where two or more people join forces to find the money required for a deposit, plus renovation costs. This could be one person funding the costs involved in buying a property, and another person carrying out the renovations. A word of warning with joint ventures though – things can go horribly wrong! Partners can fall out, one can fall ill or even die, so you must get everything in writing and only work with people that you feel you can trust.

Angel Investors:

An Angel Investor is a person, usually a successful business man or woman who provides the capital for a business start-up or deposit money to another person in return for a share in the company or by way of an interest added loan.

Whilst Angel Investors are a viable option when you are starting up in a property investment business, you do have to look carefully into your contract. Many often demand 50% of your business in return for their initial capital, so always get financial advice.

Bridging Loans:

A bridging loan is a short-term loan. I don't tend to recommend using one as a means to getting a deposit because the emphasis is on 'short-term' and you stand to pay very high interest rates if you fail to pay the loan back on time. Many property developers/ investors use a bridging loan when they need access to money quickly for a renovation project for example, but they know that they can pay the loan back before the payment deadline. This is an option that you could use to find a deposit if for example you are owed money, such as a redundancy pay out and are sure that you can pay it back in time. Most banks offer bridging loans, but it really is designed as a short-term loan only.

The Importance of a Financial Advisor/Mortgage Broker

It is quite possible for you to find a suitable lender for a property on your own, but with the financial world changing so rapidly we would advise you to seek professional advice in the form of a financial advisor or mortgage broker.

The reason for this is that financing mortgages is a minefield when it comes to the many lenders out there, their rates and criteria. Whilst you could do the research for this by yourself, it will take you many, many hours trawling through different lenders' rates.

Many first-time investors automatically go to their bank to see if they can get a mortgage. Whist you might think this is the logical answer, a professional financial advisor or mortgage broker will have access to the best deals and all the information at their fingertips.

As with stocks and shares and other investments, interest rates can and do vary on a daily basis, depending on how the economics are forecast. A financial advisor/mortgage broker will know instantly who is the best lender for you.

Jason Whitehead from Vitality Mortgages Ltd and financial advisor for this book, has been my financial advisor from the word go and I wouldn't have been able to get as far as I have without Jason's help, advice, knowledge, and years of experience.

You can expect to pay anything from £200 - £800 for a mortgage broker to get you a mortgage. Some brokers, especially those working on long-term investment projects, such as multiple buys, and bigger purchases may charge you a percentage. Just remember though, cheaper does not necessarily mean better. Some of the cheaper brokers, with estate agents, for example, may only have access to a handful of lenders and only work with a select few.

In the UK, the FCA (Financial Conduct Authority) regulates mortgage brokers and anyone advising you of financial information, such as mortgages, must adhere to the FCA's code of practice.

Financial advisors need to be qualified with one of the FCA recognised qualification CeMAP, Cert Ma, Cert Cii (MP), BA (Hons) Business & Finance, MAQ BA to name but a few, so always check how qualified your mortgage advisor is.

You can check that an individual or a firm are FCA authorized by searching them on the register https://register.fca.org.uk/

Try to find out about the type of mortgages they have handled in the past and that these match your circumstances.

Because the aim of this book is designed at those investors who want to invest in more than one property, it will benefit you to find a broker/financial advisor who you can trust to work with for the long term, not just a one-off deal.

Most financial advisors or mortgage brokers will offer a free consultation to help you work out whether you can get a buy-to-let mortgage and what the best option is for you. It's in their interest to help you find the right lender at an affordable rate. They are the professionals who do this day in day out, so let them help you.

A good place for reference is: https://moneyfacts.co.uk/mortgages/guides/

Try looking at websites such as Unbiased and Vouched For, which are independent review websites and see what your broker's clients say about them.

Don't try to tackle the world of finance on your own unless you're familiar with financial information. You will find that your time is better spent on other things and a good advisor will pay dividends when you're buying a property.

Chapter Three

Finding the Right Property

There's a strange thing within the world of estate agents and realtors that the best time to buy a property is during the spring or autumn. No one knows where this odd assumption has come from, but it's false. Properties sell the whole year round, so don't think you have to wait until a specific time of the year to find a property. In fact, properties that have been on the market for more than six months will often be reduced in price because estate agents will want to sell them. If they don't; they don't make any commission.

It's important to remember that there are plenty of properties out there and that often when a property says it's been sold, the sale can fall through. No property is legally sold until contracts are exchanged between the two parties, so it always pays to keep an eye on a 'sold' property because if a sale doesn't go through the seller may be willing to reduce the price just to get rid of it.

There are many reasons why a sale might not go through:

- A surveyor might undervalue the property.
- The buyer might not be able to get a mortgage.
- The buyer might have changed their mind at the last minute.
- The mortgage lender may have changed their mind at the last minute and refuse to lend.

So always ask the estate agent selling the property to keep you in mind if a sale does fall through.

Estate Agents:

Mention estate agents and the majority of people will roll their eyes and have a story to tell you about them! The reason for this is because they do tend to have a bit of a reputation for telling half-truths about a property. However, if you bear this in mind and accept that they are trying to sell you something with some of the oldest tricks in the book, it makes the whole cat-and-mouse game a bit easier.

One of the tricks many estate agents use is with their visual images. In this day and age when photos can be manipulated with wide lenses, cropping and soft lighting, photos of a property can and often are very misleading and that third bedroom turns out to be a room you couldn't swing a mouse in, let alone a cat.

Floor plans can also be inaccurate and are often accompanied by a disclaimer stating that they are 'for illustrative purposes only,' meaning they are in no way accurate to the actual property.

And descriptions of a property can be way off on the particulars! A six-foot square area at the back of the house can also be described as a 'small private garden'. Small properties will be described as bijou or cosy and very often a property might still be advertised as for sale but is in the process of completion with another buyer. Some estate agents do this deliberately so that they can show you another property on their books that they're trying to sell.

Viewing Properties:

The first rule of thumb when buying an investment property is to remember, **YOU ARE NOT GOING TO BE LIVING IN IT!** Far too many first-time investors (and I was one of them) view a property from the perspective of what *they* would like to live in. They look at the area – from their own perspective, they look at the décor of a property – from their perspective. They look at the layout – from their perspective. **YOU ARE NOT GOING TO BE LIVING IN IT!** So, stop looking at it as if you are.

What you personally think about a particular property

shouldn't factor into buying it. What should, however, is the following:

The Property:

For a lender to lend on a property, that property must be a solid permanent construction, so trying to get a mortgage for a mobile caravan or a wooden lodge, for example, will prove very difficult.

A solid, permanent construction is classed as a flat/apartment, a house, or a combination of, such as a house converted into flats. You are buying this property as a long-term investment that you can rent out to a tenant.

When viewing an investment property there are a few initial things to consider:

- Are there any visible signs of damp or mould?
- Are there any signs of internal/external cracks on the walls?
- Is the 3rd bedroom really adequate for a bedroom?
- Are there any communal areas such as a shared drive or hallway, and if so, who is responsible for maintenance and repairs?
- Are there any signs of subsidence? These will be long, diagonal cracks on the external walls and occasionally internally if the plaster has blown. In addition to this, the floors may be slopping, windows misaligned or difficult to open, the skirting boards coming away from the wall).
- Do the windows open and close correctly? Are they up to building regulations?
- What heating system is installed and when?
- When was the boiler installed and last serviced?
- What is the energy rating? As of 2020, all rented properties must have an energy rating of E or above.

- When were gas and electrical appliances last checked?
- Is the wiring in a property up to building regulations? As of April 2020, all new tenancies have to have an electrical check certificate by law.
- Always look at the roof of a property. If it bows, there is a problem. If it's a flat roof, has it been correctly protected?

When you are buying a property to rent out, it's important to remember that you are responsible for any defects, not your tenant. Of course, if a property isn't up to a rentable standard, but you still think it has potential and are willing to put in the work to get it up to standard, by all means put in an offer. I've bought many properties that have required renovations and in one case, a complete rebuild. We'll cover this in more detail later in the book.

Always look at a property from a business point of view. Is that property going to be easy to let out? How much are repairs going to cost? Are there any ground rent or maintenance charges to pay? (usually flats or leasehold properties). Is the property going to require a lot of building work? Is there anything that will limit your rental market – for example, it's in a high-rise block of flats without a lift, so it won't appeal to the elderly or someone with young children.

The Area:

Where a property is situated tends to get overlooked a bit by investors, but it's quite important to look at the area to give yourself an idea of your potential tenant. If your property is in the middle of nowhere with no access to public transport, schools or shops, your market for a tenant will be very different to a property in the middle of a town.

Spend a couple of days, evenings and nights driving around the area to get an idea of what it's like to live there. Houses that are near to schools, shops, parks, and public transport are the best for families. Flats/apartments located near a motorway or a trainline are perfect for singles or working couples. A cottage in the middle of the countryside would be ideal as a holiday let (although you do need to check with your mortgage lender if you are buying a property for a holiday let or an Airbnb).

What's the area like during the evening or at night? If it's very active during the evening, it might not be suitable for a family with small children. Fewer properties come with garages or private driveways nowadays, so what's the parking like, particularly on a weekend when more people are at home? If it's difficult to park near the property, this might put tenants off.

Is it Local to You?

The majority of first-time property investors opt for buying a property in their own town/village and it's advisable to do this for a number of reasons:

- You can easily keep an eye on your property.
- You are close by if there is a problem with the property, for example a flood.
- Your tenant can get hold of you quickly.
- You will have access to local traders should you need them.

If you live in the south of the country and buy a property in the north, it makes it difficult to keep an eye on things and you will need to hire the services of a letting agent (more about this later in the book).

Tenants want the reassurance that should their boiler breakdown in the middle of the night, or their electrics suddenly go, you can get repairs done quickly and efficiently. They don't want to be waiting for weeks when you can find time to attend the property.

It's a lot easier to carry out routine inspections if you are local to your property too.

Having said this, once you have some experience of being a property investor, you can always branch out further afield and buy properties in other areas. Another golden rule of investing in property is to always try and buy at below market value. Properties in the north of the country are significantly cheaper than those in the south and as we've seen in the first chapter, there will always be a need for rental housing wherever you buy in the country.

At the time of writing and with so many changes being forced upon landlords, many are selling up their stock of properties. Some are fed up with the legal red tape associated with buying investment properties, others don't realise just how much work is involved running a property business. According to PIMS.co.uk, (Property Information Made Simple) a website for landlords, just over a quarter of landlords are intending to sell at least one of their properties in 2020. For buyers this means that there will be an influx of cheaper properties available to buy. Most investors selling a property are happy to sell below market value. Having already made money from renting their property out, they will often just want to get rid of it as quickly as possible.

Houses Vs Flats:

Flats/Apartments

Most first-time investors begin their property portfolio by buying flats.

The benefit of buying a flat or apartment is:

- They are usually cheaper than a house, so consequently your deposit will be lower.
- The rental market for flats will always be good.
- They are easy to maintain.

- They are usually located near to towns with amenities.
- They are suitable for working people.
- They are usually maintained by a block management.

The downside of buying a flat or apartment is:

- They are rarely big enough for a family.
- Rental on flats is a lot less than you could get for a house.
- The majority of flats are leasehold.
- You usually have to pay a ground rent and maintenance charges.
- Living in such close proximity, there could be neighbour disputes.
- Flats and apartments often don't go up much in value.

My portfolio is a mix of houses and flats/apartments, although I started my property businesses by buying houses. Always check who is responsible for what when you consider buying a flat/apartment and whether there are any other costs involved before you put in an offer.

Houses

The benefit of buying a house is:

- At the time of writing, many houses are not much more expensive than a flat/apartment.
- You can demand a much higher rental income.
- Houses increase much quicker in value than apartments.
- Houses are perfect for families.
- If your house is in an area for good schools, shops, and transport, you will always have a tenant – usually a long-term one.
- House tenants tend to stay longer than flat tenants.

The downside of buying a house is:

- You are responsible for any repairs or maintenance on your property.
- A house usually costs more than a flat/apartment, so your deposit will be higher.
- Tenants can sometimes sublet rooms without your knowledge.
- Criminal activity, such as growing cannabis, could be happening in your house.
- It can be harder to evict a tenant if they are a family.

Buying a property for the rental market is very different to buying one for yourself, so you need to look at it from a business perspective. The property might not be something that you would personally like to live in, but you need to look at it from the view of its rental potential. Is it going to be something that you can easily rent out? Look at the current rental availability in the area. Is there a shortage of good rental properties there? Is it an area where new businesses are being introduced? Is it local to schools?

Leaseholds and Freeholds:

When you buy a property, it will come with either a freehold or a leasehold attached to it. The majority of houses are freehold which means that once you buy it, you own the property and the land that it is built on, plus any fencing, outbuildings such as a shed, etc. So, if you were to knock it down, you would be entitled to rebuild on the land that the original building was on (subject to planning permission).

The majority of flats and apartments are purchased as a leasehold. This means that although you own the flat or apartment, you do not own the land that it is built upon. When you buy a leasehold property, it means that you own the lease for a fixed period of time (usually 99 – 125 years). This indicates for that amount of time you are allowed the use of the property you have purchased. At any point that you wish to sell that property, the rest of the lease transfers to the new buyer.

When you buy a leasehold, the person/company that owns the freehold becomes your landlord and is responsible for the maintenance of the structure of the property. You will usually have to pay a cost towards this, known as a maintenance charge – usually once or twice a year with the other leaseholders.

Freeholders of a property have been known to increase their maintenance charges annually, but the government have stepped in to ensure these are fair and appropriate to leaseholders.

Occasionally, a property will be sold with a cross-over lease. This is usually when there are only two apartments, such as a ground floor and a top floor, in a single property. Cross-over leases mean that you and the other flat owner have your own lease to your individual property, but you also equally own the freehold to the whole property and any maintenance issues are split 50/50 between both parties. So, if there is for example a problem with the roof, both owners agree to share the costs. Often both flat owners will share one building insurance policy.

Your solicitor will always check the leasehold on a property as part of their searches and make sure that it is fair to you, the buyer.

Chapter Four

Buying A Property

Yields

Once you have ticked all the boxes on a property you think has good rental potential, you need to work out the financial potential on the property. Assuming you have decided that the property you're interested in is in a good rental area, you need to work out what is known as your yield. This is the total gross income you will get from renting your property out and is a must for any property investor because it will tell you whether your investment is going to be a worthy one in terms of income.

To find out how much rent you can charge on a particular property will depend on the area your property is in, so check on property websites to see what you could charge.

To work out your yield ...

- Work out what your annual income will be for that property (12 x your monthly rent).
- Divide this figure by the property's value.
- Multiply that figure by 100.

This will give you your gross yield as a percentage.

For example, if you bought a property for £150,000 and your expected rental income was £7,500/annum, you would divide £7,500 by £150,000, then multiply that by 100, giving you a 5% yield.

If your annual rental income was £12,000, and the property was valued at £200,000, your rental yield would be 6%.

Anything over 5% is considered a good investment because this gives you room for dealing with times when you might be without a tenant for a short period of time or you might be required to do some work on your property. A smaller yield will make your income smaller and your budget tighter, so it always pays to take this into account when you purchase a property. It's a pointless exercise if your rental income is only just covering your mortgage payments.

Remember, this is your gross yield. This does not take into account any insurance/maintenance/running costs you might incur for your property. Some investors add this into their calculations by deducting a percentage of their annual rental income, but I tend to find it can be difficult to estimate how much maintenance an individual property will cost.

Stamp Duty:

At the time of writing, you have to pay Stamp Duty (SD) on any property exceeding £125,000, regardless. If you already own a property, you will be subject to SD even if it costs less than £125,000, because it is classed as a second property. You have to take this into account when you are buying a property to rent out. You will pay the SD on completion and it will be included in your solicitor's final bill. For more information visit https://www.gov.uk/stamp-duty-land-tax/residential-property-rates where you will find a SD calculator which will tell you exactly how much you will have to pay.

Let the Games Begin!

Assuming you're happy with the yield your property will generate, it's now time to play a game with the estate agent selling the property!

It's really important to bear in mind that the buying of a property is a business transaction and those involved are doing so with the goal of making money: The seller wants to get as much money as possible from the sale of their property; the estate agent also wants to get as much money from the sale of the property because that increases their commission and is how they make their money, and you want to get a good deal on the property you are buying, so that you can earn enough money out of property investment to not have to work again.

As an industry, estate agents have a bad reputation, but this is only because people don't see that it is business and whilst they might bemuse you with their sales tricks – and lies – and yes, many do tell lies, such as they have had a lot of interest in a property, or that you will have to act quick because someone else has put in an offer. They do this because these tactics work. Tell a potential buyer that they are competing with another 25 buyers and they are not going to offer below the asking price and might even increase their offer.

I've had agents tell me that another buyer has offered on a property in a bid to get me to increase my offer, only to come back to me and say that the other buyer has pulled out. I've had low offers declined, only for them to come back six weeks later asking if I'm still interested in buying the property at my original offer. More recently, I had an estate agent tell me that the seller of a property I was buying was thinking of pulling out of the sale because my solicitor was taking too long to complete. Little did they know that I know the seller and he never said he was thinking of pulling out or had any intention to.

If you look at this process of purchasing a property as a game and take what the estate agent tells you with a pinch of salt, you will have a much easier time and always remember, it's business.

The longer you are in the business of buying property, the more estate agents will respect you and take you seriously. They will stop with the games and will often contact you prior to a property going on the market.

I have a few estate agents who know what I'm looking for in terms of a rental property and will often contact me with what's coming on the market, knowing that if I'm interested, they will secure a quick sale for their seller.

Making an Offer:

Estate agents will always inflate the value of a property by a few thousand pounds because they know that when buyers offer on a property it will usually be slightly below the asking price. I've rarely offered the full asking price on a property unless it's been something that I know is going to give me a good return.

Do your research on a property prior to making an offer on it. How long has it been on the market? Don't rely on the estate agent to tell you this. It may have only been on their books for two weeks, but it may have been with another agent for two years. Property websites such as Rightmove and Zoopla often list when a property was first put up for sale. For a few pounds you can get a lot of information about a property on the Land Registry, including when a property was sold and for how much.

Ask the estate agent why the owner is selling. If it's due to a life change, such as a death, divorce or relocating, they will usually want a quick sale and will be more open to offers. It's as much in the estate agent's interest as the sellers to sell a property quickly and if you make it known you're a property investor, this can go in your favour. Whilst we don't want to encourage anyone to make money out of another person's misfortune, if you can equip yourself with some background information, you could be the one who profits and at the same time help the seller out by buying their property from them.

It's important to stick to your original offer. Don't be swayed into the game of going back and forth with offers and counter offers. This is a classic estate agent game to try and get a few more thousand for their client and their commission. It's a tricky one because the estate agent is working for both you and the vendor, so there's a slight conflict of interest in any sale. Remember, there are plenty of other properties to buy and there always will be! You're not buying your forever home; you're buying it as an investment to make money from.

You don't need to justify your offer, just tell the estate agent the amount you wish to offer and ask him/her to present it to their client.

Offer Accepted:

Assuming your offer has been accepted, you will then receive a letter of memorandum from the estate agent, detailing your acceptance, the amount and asking for your details.

These details will include who is buying the property, address, ID requests, and who your lender and solicitor will be.

Many estate agents will ask for a mortgage in principle from your lender prior to putting in your offer to the seller. You may not have this at this stage and it often makes buyers panic that they will lose a property on this basis. This is not so and is another fib estate agents try to use against buyers, assuming that if you're serious about buying a property you would already have this in place. It is however a bit of a chicken and egg scenario: you can't get a mortgage in principle on a property you haven't yet seen, and some estate agents won't put your offer forwards without one.

If an estate agent tells you that they need this piece of paper prior to putting in your offer, ask your financial advisor or mortgage broker to draft one up for you. They will already know which lenders will be willing to lend to you in principle.

I always find it helpful to type up a pre-prepared copy of my personal details and that of my financial advisor, solicitor and copies of my ID, just to give the estate agent something to work on and get the ball rolling. It tends to keep them quiet for a few days while I get things moving with the finances.

If you're lucky enough to have a financial advisor like I do who is happy to deal with any queries solicitors or estate agents have, all the better. It pays to have someone in your court who you can refer to, for example, if your lender is taking their time to get paperwork to your solicitor.

Once your offer has been accepted by the seller, it's important to remember that any party can pull out of the sale up until the point of completion of the sale. In the UK, the sale process takes between eight and 12 weeks to go through. Contrary to popular belief, gazumping, which is when another buyer offers more on a property you have already verbally agreed to buy, is not illegal in the UK. However, most reputable estate agents don't encourage this sort of behaviour.

You can ask your solicitor to write up a 'lock-in' agreement. This is a legally binding agreement between the seller and the buyer that they both agree not to negotiate with any other parties within a fixed period, allowing the buyer to arrange their mortgage etc., without fear of being gazumped. This usually comes at a cost of around 2% of the price of the property so that if either party decides to back out of the sale without good reason, the other party will be responsible for paying for the inconvenience of the sale not going through. It's quite rare for this to be implemented though.

When your offer has been accepted, your financial advisor will find the right lender at the best rate and appoint a solicitor on your behalf. You can of course appoint your own solicitor, but many lenders will only use certain conveyancing solicitors who are on their panel, so it's wise to check with your lender as to whether they will work with the solicitor you want to use.

This is why it is so important and easier to use the services of a good financial advisor or mortgage broker because they know the industry inside out and will save you a lot of time and money.

At this stage there is no point in trying to chase things up or speed things along. It's important to remember you are not the only person in the world buying a property and things such as searches, flood reports, exchange of solicitor's information etc., all take time.

The average time it takes for a property to be sold in the UK is between eight and 12 weeks. That's if there are no complications, such as a link in a chain being broken. This is something that estate agents seem to forget and often try to hurry the process along, despite knowing full well how long some solicitors take to answer queries, run searches, etc.

A few times I've had veiled threats from estate agents that their seller is going to pull out of a sale because the process is taking too long. Despite telling them that I'm fine with that, no seller has ever pulled out from a sale – and if they do, there are plenty of other properties on the market. You won't lose any money if you or a seller decides to pull out of an agreement.

As long as you have your deposit ready, or you know it will be available by the time of completion, you have your mortgage offer and a solicitor acting for you, you can sit back and allow everyone else to get on with their jobs.

Solicitors:

It's impossible to buy a property without the help of a solicitor. Even a cash buyer has to employ a solicitor to legalise the paperwork and change the deeds of a property. A good solicitor will ensure not only the purchase goes through but will also check things such as access, parking rights and in the case of a flat purchase, who is responsible for what areas.

So, where do you find a good solicitor to represent you? Most first-time investors look for a local conveyancing solicitor and hire them, or their estate agent recommends the one they use. Whilst this is a good option in terms of being able to visit them to sign documents or keep a close eye on the process, some local solicitors are small firms, with many other cases to deal with.

I used a local solicitor for my first purchase and because he was a one-man firm, it took forever to get him to work on my case. His office was never open and my only means of contact was Joyce, his fiercely protective secretary, who often forgot to pass my messages on to him.

Most mortgage advisors will have access to several solicitors that they have worked with in the past and as I've mentioned before, they will know which ones will work with which lenders. This is not to say that a solicitor who comes recommended will be a perfect match. I've had to change solicitors several times when I've bought a property that has had to be complete by a specified time and the firm has been less then competent.

Buying a property involves a lot of legalities and can cost you a lot of money if your solicitor hasn't done their job properly. If you do have to complain about a solicitor, you should contact the Solicitors Regulation Authority (SRA) or the Legal Ombudsman.

Valuations and Surveys:

A mortgage lender won't give you a mortgage without the property having a valuation and a survey conducted on it. The property might look perfect, but it could also have hidden problems such as no damp course, a leaking roof, rotting timbers, subsidence.

I once offered on a three-bed Victorian house only to find that when the surveyor and valuation report came back, they had negative-valued it due to there being no damp course, meaning they could not put any value on it. My mortgage lender refused to lend me the money on it.

A valuation and survey will cost anything from £200 - £400, but it is money well spent to give you the peace of mind that the property you are buying is not going to fall down or be plagued with problems. It also tells you and your lender what the real market value of your property it.

Your mortgage broker/lender/solicitor will instruct a valuation on your behalf. Occasionally a valuer might under-value your property. Sometimes valuers only do a basic check on a property and compare it to other similar properties in the area to find out the value of a property. I've had this happen to me twice and both times we've challenged the valuation and won our case.

Obviously if a valuer under-values your property, this can have an effect on the amount of money your mortgage lender will lend you and you could end up being told that you will have to increase your deposit.

Valuers always have a 10% margin of any valuation, but if you feel that your property has been significantly under-valued, you can contact the Royal Institution of Chartered Surveyors and make an official complaint.

A word of caution: if you are buying a property above shops or near to a petrol station and your valuer mentions this, your mortgage lender might retract their offer in principle. Lenders prefer minimum risk properties and will always have a risk assessment for any property that isn't a straightforward two-up-two-down on a residential street.

Purpose built flats above shops are usually safer bets than a property that has been converted to a flat above a shop for example.

Valuers will take into account noise pollution, parking, crime and risk to a property when they assess it. They will also consider how easy the property would be to resell should it have to be repossessed.

BUYING AT AUCTION

Buying a property using an estate agent is not the only way that you can purchase a buy-to-let property. There are many good properties that come up for auction every day and if you know what you're doing, you can pick up a good bargain. I bought my very first property at auction and it was a great experience for me.

Finding Auction Properties:

You can find out what properties are coming up for auction and when by contacting your local estate agent. Some run auctions themselves, others put their auction properties in the hands of a property auctioneer. Auctions are usually advertised a few months in advance, to enable buyers the opportunity to view a property and look at the legal pack, which is always advisable, no matter how good a deal something seems on paper. Many auctions are carried out in a hotel or other such local venue and it's not as scary as you first think.

Viewing a Property:

As with any major purchase, it's important that you view an auction property prior to bidding on it. We've all heard of the stories of people rocking up to an auction, buying a property that they haven't viewed and making a huge profit on it. This rarely happens in real life.

When you buy a property at auction, you are buying it 'as seen', so you can't go back for a refund if you discover that there's no ceiling in the property that you've just bought. Which is why it is so important to not only view the property but also read through the legal pack that comes with every property.

The legal pack will tell you what you are buying and whether there are any clauses within the purchase, such as who owns the freehold and whether there are any other legal conditions attached to buying the property.

When you arrange to view a auction property it's always worth asking a builder or someone in the construction trade to go along with you. That crack down the wall might just be settlement, but it might also be subsidence. Take a step ladder with you so that you can look in the loft. Lofts, attics, and basements can all hide problems, even though the rest of the property might look in good condition.

It's always advisable to view a property at least twice. There are things that you might miss the first time around. And view it at different times of the day – that two-bed semi might look fine during the day but the alleyway at the back might also be a haven for drug dealers by night.

Properties That Come Up for Auction:

Properties that come up for auction are often ones that the vendors need a quick sale on. This might be because it is part of a deceased's estate, or they have tried the usual avenues of selling a property and it just hasn't sold. You will often find repossessed properties at auctions too. These are properties that have been repossessed by the bank or mortgage lender because the owner has fallen into arrears with their mortgage. Some properties that come up for auction are properties that a mortgage lender won't lend on, such as a non-concrete building. Always go careful if buying a property like this because whilst you may easily be able to rent it out, you will have a much more difficult time should you ever wish to resell it in its current condition.

Guide Price:

Every property that comes up in an auction will have a guide price attached to it. This price gives you an idea of what the auctioneer expects the property to sell for. The guide price is just that – a guide, and the auctioneer sets it to be within 10% higher or lower of an expected sale. So, if for example, the guide price on a property is set at £150,000, the auctioneer expects it to sell between £135,000 and £165,000. Obviously if there is a lot of interest in a property, the final price can exceed their estimation.

Setting a Budget and Funding:

It's very important that you set a budget when buying an auction property. It's very easy to get carried away when the auctioneer increases the price by just £500 every time another person bids on a property. But those extra £500 quickly add up when you're competing with another bidder.

It's also important to remember that when buying at an auction there are fees for both the buyer and the seller. A seller will be expected to pay a fee the same as if they sold to an estate agent. The buyer can expect to also pay a fee to the auction house, often referred to as an 'admin fee', which can range from £500 - £2000, depending on the property.

This is why it is so important to have a budget and to stick to it. Some buyers offset the costs of the legal pack to the buyer as well, so you need to check with the auction house prior to thinking about bidding on a property.

Properties bought at auction are usually 'purchase on the day' properties, so you need to make sure you have the money in place before you bid, and the hammer goes down. Once the hammer drops, you and the seller are legally obliged to honour the purchase.

You will be required to pay the auction house 10% of the price of the property there and then at the auction and then you will have 28 days to complete the purchase. You will also need to have proof that you have the rest of the money ready, so it's very important to have your funding sorted before you think about buying at an auction.

If you don't have actual cash in the bank, you will need to get in touch with a financial advisor about the different options. One such option is what's known as a bridging loan. This is a short-term loan option that many investors use. It is also a risky option. The emphasis on a bridging loan is that it is a *short-term* loan. If you miss the deadline payment you will end up paying huge amounts back in interest, so you need to be 100% sure that any renovations won't run over. Bridging loans are ideal if you have a mortgage in principle (a statement from the lender telling you they will agree to lend money to you), but you can't get hold of the money before the auction.

The Auction Process:

Property auctions are run all over the country and vary from being held in hotel conference rooms, to purpose-built auction houses and village halls. They usually consist of a room with several chairs laid out for prospective buyers and desks at the front for the auctioneer and any admin staff.

Estate agents selling a property on behalf of their client will often be there to answer any questions and you will be given a brochure or a list of all the properties that are coming up for auction that day.

A misconception of property auctions is that friends of the seller are planted there to bid on their mate's property in order to increase the price. This doesn't happen. Imagine if your friend outbids a real buyer and ends up having to buy the property!

The auctioneer will introduce him/herself and start with the first property, known as a Lot. They will talk a bit about the property and inform the audience of the guide price. It's very important that you don't begin the bidding. Now, I know you'll answer, 'well someone has to start it' and yes, that is true, but if no one puts their hand up at the first price, the auctioneer will reduce it slightly, usually by around £500 - £1000. This gives you that extra money to start with because the price has already been lowered.

Once someone begins bidding on the property you're interested in, hold on until you get an idea of who you are bidding against. Remember, everyone there will also have a budget to stick to. It's very exciting to put your hand up and bid against another person, just don't get too carried away – remember, you want to make a profit on this and that means getting a property for less than you would normally pay.

Depending on the number of other bidders, depends on how successful you will be with your bid, but once that hammer goes down on your bid, it's one of the greatest feelings in the world – it's also one of the most terrifying!

Prior to attending an auction and buying a property I was interested in I contacted the estate agent selling the property and I offered the guide price they had set for the auction. The estate agent asked the seller if he would be interested, rather than taking the property to auction. He refused, even though I had the cash in the bank and didn't need to get a loan and it would have been a relatively quick and straightforward sale. The seller wanted to see if he could get more by selling it at auction.

On the night of the auction there was one other bidder interested in the property. The auctioneer started the price at 10% lower than the guide price. My competitor bid first, but then stopped bidding after I bid, resulting in me having the final bid – at the original price I had offered the estate agent. If the seller had accepted my offer in the first place, he wouldn't have had to pay any auctioneer fees.

When you have secured your bid, you will be asked to go to the admin desk and provide them with the 10% deposit, the admin/auction fee and proof of funds. Obviously, you should have this prior to going to the auction. You will then have 28 days in which to transfer the rest of the cost of the property – plus your stamp duty and solicitor's fees.

Occasionally an auction property won't make the minimum guide price the auctioneer has set on it. If this happens, the auctioneer will pull the property from the auction. Whilst this can be disappointing, it does mean that you can then contact the estate agent the following day and put in an offer. If the seller is desperate to sell, you could get yourself a real bargain.

Chapter Five

Now What?

Finally, you have the keys to your new property! Now you need to consider carefully what to do next. For this part of the book, I have divided this section into two parts – the first is designed for those of you who have bought a ready-to-go property and are all ready to get a tenant in as soon as is viably possible. The second section is for those that have purchased a property that needs some renovations.

SECTION ONE
YOUR PROPERTY IS READY TO GO

FINDING A TENANT:

Seriously, I could write a whole book on my experience of tenants – the good, the bad and the downright nasty, and I'll touch on a few of the mistakes I've made over the years of being a professional landlord later in the book.

The most important thing to consider once you've purchased your BTL property is that you get a tenant in as quickly and as swiftly as possible. Your mortgage lender is not going to wait for you to find someone to pay the rent, which will in turn pay your mortgage on the property, so you do need to act quickly on this.

You may already know a family member, a friend or a friend of a friend who desperately needs somewhere to rent and think this is an ideal solution – **DON'T DO IT!** I've only once let one of my properties to a friend and it didn't end well when he thought that because we were friends, he could consistently be late with his rent. I also made the mistake of not asking him for a deposit because he assured me, (because we were friends) that he would keep the house in the same immaculate condition I let it out to him. He didn't – he acquired three dogs who ruined all the carpets, scratched the doors, and tore up the Victorian parquet flooring.

As tempting as it is to allow a family member or friend to rent from you, please don't be persuaded to do this. You, like me, could be faced with thousands of pounds worth of damage, broken promises, out of pocket and the loss of a friendship.

At the time of writing, (Spring 2020) The National Residential Landlords Association state that there are currently more tenants than properties. The demand outweighs the supply, so you will always find a tenant and there are many ways to source one that is going to be a delight, rather than a disaster.

USING AN AGENT:
There are many letting agents out there, some who are solely letting agents, others are sister companies of estate agents. I've used a lettings agent for the majority of my portfolio and have stayed with the same one for the past six years.

From my own experience, I would recommend having a lettings agent if you have more than one property or are looking at expanding your portfolio. The reason I say this is because lettings is a minefield of legalities that a professional letting agent can help you with. Just as I said before, you can manage your mortgages on your own without using the skills of a financial advisor or broker, and you can manage your properties on your own without the need of a letting agent. But it is hard work and you do need to keep up to date with the ever-changing legislation relating to landlords and tenants. Plus, if you are considering having a lot of rental properties, your passive income will become a full-time job if you decide to manage all your properties on your own.

Some portfolio landlords have formed their own lettings company and employed experienced staff to manage their properties for them, so this is something you might think about at a later date.

As it now stands, landlords/letting agents are no longer allowed to charge tenants for viewings, reference checks, credit checks or anything else relating to the right to rent a property. You will have to pay for these yourself, or your letting agent will charge for the service. This can get quite costly and unfortunately some letting agents have abused this by charging far more than necessary for these checks. I know of one agent who charged a landlord three times the cost of obtaining an EPC certificate, which actually costs around £50 if you do it yourself online. Since the changes, it actually costs me almost the equivalent of one month's rent on a property for my letting agent to carry out the necessary checks to get a good tenant signed up for your property.

The NRLA (National Residential Landlords Association) and PIMS (Property Information Made Simple) websites, specifically designed for landlords, offer new tenancy services at a fraction of the price that a letting agent will charge you.

The advantage of having a letting agent is that they act as the go-between for you and your tenant. The more properties you have in your portfolio, the less time you have to attend to each and every tenant's request/demand.

A letting agent will set up everything from interviewing tenants to doing an inventory to moving tenants in and collecting the rent for you, which frees up more of your time to do the things you want to do. As with every industry, letting agents come in good and not so good sizes. Some will be there for you every step of the way; others will drop you the minute there's trouble looming, such as a tenant failing to pay their rent and you having to seek possession of your property through a court.

I've been fortunate that the agency I use has been pretty good to date and I'm thankful that they attend to the day-to-day business of dealing with tenant's demands so that I don't have to. We've only had one awful eviction to deal with, which got very messy, but they were there to support me when I had to take the tenants to court.

Obviously, using a letting agent doesn't come for nothing and you can expect to pay anything between 8 and 12% of your property's monthly rent if you use an agent. For me, it's a cost I'm happy to pay for peace of mind and knowing that someone else is dealing with my tenants for me. Some of my properties are rented out via my local council's Homeless Prevention Scheme, of which I talk about in more detail at the end of the book. These properties don't require a letting agent because the council do all the necessary checks etc.

Your letting agent will also have access to a range of contractors when maintenance problems arise. However, it may pay you to find your own reliable contractors because agents often add 10% onto the cost of using one of their recommended tradesmen, although they won't tell you this.

It's wise to keep a list of any work that has been done on your property because I've known some agents make up maintenance issues that never needed doing or repeating jobs which have already been attended to such as annual gas checks.

SELF-MANAGING:

Depending on your other commitments, you can of course self-manage your property. My daughters, who also work full time, manage their properties by themselves. They use a company called Open Rent to start a tenancy, who source and reference tenants prior to viewing and they will sort out the deposit and arrange the setup of rent payments, at a very reasonable cost far cheaper than a letting agent.

The advantage of self-managing is that you are in total control of everything related to your property and you are not paying any middleman to look after your property for you. The disadvantages are that you could find that your tenant is constantly calling you for repairs or queries at all hours of the day and night.

If you are intending to self-manage your properties, it pays to have a separate phone number for tenants to contact you and access to a few reliable maintenance contractors in case you need a plumber in the middle of the night.

TENANT CHECKS:

You'll be amazed at the lengths some tenants will go to get through credit and referencing checks. I've had people try to submit other people's details, passports and driving licenses before in a bid to pass through the necessary checks. I had one tenant change the date of birth on his girlfriend's passport in order to try and get past credit checks and it was only because I noticed that their date of births was identical that I picked up on it. I've had references given by tenant's friends pretending to be their current employer when they were in fact not in work. There will always be people who will hide things in the hope that they will get overlooked – and unfortunately, sometimes they do.

If you use a letting agent, they are usually skilled at detecting if a prospective tenant is genuine or if they are trying to hide something, but it always pays to do your own checks too. Regardless of whether you are self-managing or are using an agent it pays to do more than the standard reference and credit checks that are required, including finding as much information online that you can about the person who wants to rent your property. You have to remember that you are not the only landlord on an agent's books, and at the end of the day, it is your property that is being rented out.

Social media provides a useful wealth of information that you will never find on a standard reference check. There will be pictures of their holiday, their family, their work, and their pets all online and will give you a good idea of what type of person they are.

I discovered (albeit a bit too late) that one of my tenants who claimed he was a CEO of a media company was not true and he had in fact been sacked from every company that he had ever worked for. His social media accounts revealed that he and his partner were abusive, rude, and aggressive to people. They constantly fell out with neighbours and they owed thousands of pounds to different companies. It shouldn't have been a surprise to me when they decided to not pay their rent for eight months and I had to have them evicted through the courts.

I once had a tenant who was a builder and decided to take it upon himself to make alternations to one of my properties without asking me. Unfortunately, he wasn't very good at his job either, so when he left because his business went bankrupt, I was left with a house that had to be repaired. Fortunately, I had taken a deposit from him which covered some of the costs.

A while back I had a couple enquire about renting one of my properties. The feedback from the agent was that they were a nice couple without pets or children, had their own business and seemed very suitable – on paper. A quick search on social media told a very different story. They had five children between them, several pets, the business had only been set up that week and the husband hadn't worked for 10 years, despite telling my agent he worked for a charity. They also requested the garden to be re-turfed and an outdoor tap to be installed – apparently deal breakers for them. I politely declined their application.

If a prospective tenant is telling you half-truths from the start, there's a reason why, so don't be tempted to accept the first person who enquires and make sure you check every source you can from court records for CJJs to Facebook, Twitter and Instagram.

With the UK government giving more rights to tenants and less to landlords at an ever increasing rate it is important that you do everything you possibly can to get a good and reliable tenant because if you make a mistake, you will pay heavily for it and it could be months before you can evict a bad tenant.

Obviously, you cannot discriminate against a prospective tenant for sex, race, religion, culture or their employment or lack of. However, if someone doesn't tell you the truth about themselves from the beginning, this is usually a red flag that they might not be the best tenant for you.

DEPOSITS:

You should *always* ask for a deposit from your prospective tenant. This will cover any damage that might occur for the duration of their tenancy. By law you can only ask a maximum of five weeks rent to cover your deposit, so if you're charging £100/week, you can ask for a deposit of £500. Unfortunately if your tenant leaves your property in a mess, their deposit often doesn't cover the costs of repairs and maintenance, but the government have decided in their wisdom, despite not being landlords, that this is all you are allowed to take as a deposit.

Again, by law, your deposit has to lodged with The Tenancy Deposit Scheme, which is an independent holding source for tenants' deposits. This was set up because some unscrupulous landlords were keeping their tenant's deposits and not returning them.

You can lodge the deposit with The Tenancy Deposit Scheme yourself for nothing, or you can ask your letting agent to do it – they shouldn't charge you for it as it is a free service if you use their Custodial Scheme, which means the TDS hold the deposit money for you and you and your tenant both have to agree to release the deposit. Some agents have been known to use this free scheme but charge the landlord, so always check whether they are using the Custodial Scheme because they shouldn't charge you for this.

INVENTORY:

It's important to make an inventory prior to letting your property out to a new tenant. This protects you and your tenant should there be a disputing issue when they move out. To make an inventory, go to every room in the property and detail everything that is in there and the condition that it is in. This includes windows, doors, skirting boards, paint work/decoration and flooring.

Take pictures of any scratched surfaces, dents in walls etc. and list them on the inventory. This acts as your record of proof should the tenant do any damage to your property. Do the same with any outdoor spaces and take pictures of the electric, gas and water meter readings. Again, if you have an agent, they will do this for you prior to a tenant moving in.

CONTRACTS:

You contract is a legal agreement between you and your tenant. Your letting agent will have a standard contract ready, but if you wish to manage your property yourself, you can download a tenancy agreement from the National Residential Landlords Association or other landlord websites.

The majority of tenancy agreements are Assured Short Term Tenancies (AST). An AST is a property that:

- The property you rent is private
- The tenancy started on or after 15 January 1989
- The property is the tenant's main accommodation
- The landlord doesn't live in the property

A tenancy can't be an AST if:

- It began or was agreed before 15 January 1989
- The rent is more than £100,000 a year
- The rent is less than £250 a year (less than £1,000 in

London)
- It's a business tenancy or tenancy of licensed premises
- The property is a holiday let
- You let to the local council (more about this later)

Other tenancies:

There are other tenancies that aren't as common as ASTs, including:

Excluded tenancies or licences:

This applies if you live in the property you are letting and share rooms such as the kitchen and bathroom with your tenant. This comes under lodgings so you can't offer your tenant an AST.

Assured tenancies:

These are only for tenancies starting between 15 January 1989 and 27 February 1997.

Regulated tenancies:

Again, these are for tenancies starting before 15 January 1989 and are regulated by the local council.

A standard AST between the tenant and landlord is an agreement that outlines the conditions by which the landlord is willing to let their property be rented out. At the time of writing, they have to be for a minimum of six months. After that you can either extend the contract for a further six months, or you can offer a contract on a rolling periodic basis, whereby the tenant is still bound by the contract, but on a month by month basis.

In my experience, families much prefer some assurance that they are not going to lose their home and often prefer a six/12-month contract, renewed every year. As a landlord It's important to consider your tenant's point of view and how you would feel if you were renting your home.

At the time of writing, the government are talking about making tenancies longer, possibly three-year tenancies. This obviously secures a tenant who might have children in the local school or jobs in the area and gives the landlord security of knowing that their tenant is going to stay for the long term. However, as with most governmental decisions, their proposals are badly thought out. They have already made it very difficult for a landlord to evict a bad tenant, even if that tenant has withheld their rent, or damages your property. If longer tenancy terms come into effect, it could have negative consequences for landlords of dreadful tenants.

At the time of writing we are in the middle of a world pandemic and as such landlords have been banned from issuing eviction notices to tenants. This is understandable given that many tenants' employment prospects have been made insecure. However, it also means that landlords can and will lose out if a tenant fails to pay their rent. Added to this, courts have been closed and previous eviction cases have had to be postponed, meaning that it will take a long time before a landlord can legally evict a tenant and get their property back or any rental income in to pay their mortgage.

Many tenants have argued that landlords can apply for a mortgage holiday, meaning they can stop paying for their mortgage for up to three months. What these tenants don't understand is that the mortgage holiday period is added to the landlord's loan and still has to be paid back. They are not getting a free period where they don't have to pay their mortgage. In turn, the tenant is still responsible for paying that rent period, which will then count as rent arrears for a tenant.

I personally allowed some of my tenants one rent-free month and have thankfully not suffered due to the economic disaster, but other landlords have, and it will take a while before they get back on their feet again. This is another reason why it's important to have a contingency plan in place.

CLAUSES:

ASTs allow the landlord to include clauses into their contracts, so for example, if your property already has a washing machine in it, you can put in a 'white goods clause' which will exempt you from having to repair or replace any white goods products. I always advise not to include any additional furnishings in a property, such as white goods, heaters or electrical appliances that are not already part of the property. If you do, you will become responsible for these and have to have them PAT tested every year.

NOTICE:

On an AST agreement, you as the landlord, are required to give your tenant two months' notice to vacate the property and the tenant is required to give one months' notice. Again, an unfair legality concocted by the government, but a legal requirement, nonetheless.

If you wish to evict a tenant, you have to do this by issuing a Section 21 notice. A Section 21 notice is also known as a 'no fault' notice in writing to say that the landlord wishes to have their property back, but that there is no problem with the tenant. At the time of writing, the government are trying to stop the issue of Section 21 notices, believing that a lot of landlords can issue them without a good reason for evicting their tenant.

Again, this is another sign of government officialdom that doesn't actually know how renting a property works. A landlord might wish to sell their property, they might have decided they no longer wish to be a landlord or might want to live in the property themselves. Regardless of the reason why a landlord might want their property back – it is still THEIR property and whilst I am in favour of many tenants' rights, the tenant is not responsible for the mortgage; the landlord is.

ADDITIONAL INFORMATION:

You can include additional information in your contract, including what will happen should a tenant not pay their rent, redecorate without permission, run a business, keep pets, do something illegal in the property, or sub-let a room in the property. Whilst the majority of tenants are lovely people, there are a few (and I've had my fair share of them) who will assume because they pay rent, they are entitled to do what they like with your property.

I know many landlords who now include clauses that should their tenant turn out to be a bad tenant, they will inform other landlords and letting agents. Obviously, you do have to be careful with data protection, but if a tenant is willing to sign the clause, you have every right to warn other professionals about a tenant to avoid if you have a public court order verifying this. (Please see below about Data Protection).

PETS:

I know many landlords who have a strict no pets' policy when renting their properties. I have a handful of tenants who do have pets and being an animal lover, I'm happy to allow pets in some of my properties, but for the tenants who do have pets, I do include a 'Pet Clause' in my contracts, which states that any damage cause by the pet will be charged to the tenant at the end of the tenancy.

Allowing pets in your property is of course entirely up to you, but if you do, you have to be prepared that they could wreck your property and the deposit won't cover having to replace all your carpets if a pet has been allowed to go to the toilet on them.

Again, the government are currently trying to pass a law that prevents a landlord from not allowing pets in their property. Which in my opinion is just another attempt at controlling landlords and what they can and can't do with their own properties.

DATA PROTECTION:

As a landlord you are bound by Data Protection laws governed by the Information Commissioners Office as to what information you are allowed to divulge to another party. If you have an agent taking care of your property, they will be aware of what information they can and can't exchange with other parties regarding a tenant. However, some tenants will abuse this, whether you have an agent acting for you or not.

When I had to evict a tenant due to rent arrears, the tenant contacted the ICO to complain that I had shared his and his partners personal information with a third party. As my property was with a letting agent, he first tried to get the letting agent into trouble, but as they have a big legal team, he was unsuccessful, so he tried to come direct to me.

He was right, I had shared his information – to the court, for non-payment of rent. The court found in my favour, evicted him from the property and ordered him to repay the outstanding rent, plus my court costs.

However, the ICO office failed to check the factual information and only considered the tenant's complaint; that I had shared his information – not who I had shared it with. After several months of the ICO threatening me with a £4,000 fine, I eventually received a letter to say that the case was closed.

The letter also asked me to contact the tenant to assure him that I hadn't disclosed his personal information. As I was still trying to track down the new address of the tenant to chase up the rent arrears, I asked the ICO to let me have his new address – they sent me another letter giving the address of my own property – the property he used to rent from me. You really couldn't make it up!

Having spent some time investigating the ICO, I discovered this is not the first time that they have done this kind of thing to a landlord or a small business. If you feel that you have been treated unfairly by the ICO, ask a solicitor to look into the case because it seems that they often take these cases at face value and do not look at the defence case at all.

INSURANCE:

When you purchase a property, your lender will require you to take out buildings insurance prior to releasing the funds. This isn't as expensive as you might think – around £200/year to cover a property.

I'd advise you also take out landlords' insurance to cover and damage that might occur to your property by your tenants.

Again, this is not terribly expensive, but will prove worthy in the long run. I have all my properties covered with a landlord insurance company and I'm so glad I have. In the space of one weekend, a cottage I own had the roof tiles come off the roof in a storm, someone drove into the pillars outside the property and another person drove his tractor through the fence! It cost thousands of pounds to repair, but thankfully the insurance company paid for it, aside from a £250 excess.

Recently one of my tenants left the taps on in her home, flooding the bathroom, which in turn flooded the ceiling below, which then fell down into the kitchen. Again, I was thankfully insured for the damage and my insurance company paid for it.

Accidents happen and sometimes tenants don't treat their home with the respect they would if they had bought it themselves, so always get your property insured. Some insurers will specialise in landlord insurance or multi-property insurance schemes.

DÉCOR:

We will touch more on this in Section Two of the book, but it's important to remember that when you buy a property to rent out, you are not going to be living in it and your taste in décor may be very different to that of your tenant.

With this in mind, it's advisable to keep the decoration to

the bare minimum. By this, I mean, clean and neutral colours, such as white or magnolia walls, so that any marks left by your tenant can be easily repainted.

Even magnolia, which is the most popular colour in a rental property, can be a bit of a pain when trying to match the paint if you can't get the same brand! So always make sure you buy a spare tin of paint when purchasing for your property, because chances are the brand you want in 18 months' time will no longer be available!

I try to steer away from wallpapering any room in a rental property because again, it can be hard to match the paper if your tenant accidentally rips it, or their child draws all over it.

When I first started renting out properties, I would put nice art on the walls, rugs in every room, towels in the bathrooms – I would even leave flowers and a bottle of wine out for every new tenant. Over time I've learned that this is not just a waste of money, it's not necessary.

Tenants wants to put their own mark on their home and unfortunately, some tenants do not treat your property as they would if they had bought it themselves. Walls get damaged, doors get broken and gardens get overgrown, so you are wasting your money by painting all your walls in Farrow and Ball, Cinder Rose and installing a swan water feature in the garden.

Keep to the basics – white ceilings and either white or magnolia trade emulsion. Paint skirtings in white satin rather than gloss, because it lasts longer, and gloss tends to go yellow after a while. Flooring should be kept to dark, heard wearing carpets or good quality, tongue and groove wood flooring. Try to avoid vinyl flooring where possible because it can get ripped easily when furniture is moved around.

KEEPING RECORDS:

Whether you have a single property or a number of properties, it's important to keep records of everything to do with your property. I keep a storage box, plus a folder for every property I own. This means whenever I need to find a document or a tenancy agreement, I know exactly where to locate it.

I keep another file for receipts and invoices relating to my properties and I send these to my accountant every month, simply because I find it easier than doing it once every six/12 months.

Even if you only have one rental property, treat it as a business right from the start. It's all too easy to put things to one side and think, I'll do that later, then discover you can't find the document you were looking for.

LANDLORD RESPONSIBILITIES:

Because laws regarding anyone renting out a property change so quickly, please refer to the government's website on the latest landlord responsibilities at https://www.gov.uk/renting-out-a-property.

As a quick reminder, as a landlord you must ensure the health and safety of your tenants in your property. This includes having an EPC certificate, an annual gas safety check and, as of April 2020, a five yearly electrical check. You must also have a carbon monoxide detector (if you have any gas appliances) and smoke alarms in your property and these must also be checked regularly.

It is your responsibility to attend to any issues with your property. If it is an emergency such as a leaking pipe, you are allowed to enter your property immediately. However, if you just wish to check on your property, you must by law give your tenant 48 hours' notice and get their permission. Remember, although it is your house, it is also their home.

TENANT RESPONSIBILITIES:

You should outline your tenant's responsibilities in your contract, but as a basic, tenants must treat your property with respect and not damage it in any way. If you allow them to redecorate, it should be on the understanding that the property is returned to its original condition if they move out.

TENANT DISPUTES:

I could write a whole book on disputes between landlords and tenants! You only have to see how popular shows such as 'Nightmare Tenants, Slum Landlords' and 'Don't Pay, We'll Take It Away' are to see that it is a problem that every landlord will face at some time in their career.

This is another reason why I recommend getting an agent. Yes, it costs you around 10 – 12% of your rental income every month, but your agent will act as a go-between, between you and your tenant and will often sort out any disputes between you.

This system usually works well, but it's very important to tell your agent not to divulge your personal details such as your address or phone number to your tenants. Tenants must always go direct to the agent if there is a problem. Unfortunately, sometimes things don't always work out the way they are supposed to. I've been threatened with violence, had death threats, and had abusive phone calls and messages from both tenants and tradesmen during my time as a landlord and property investor.

WHEN THINGS GO WRONG:

I've thankfully only had one really bad experience with tenants, and I hope never to repeat the experience again!

A young couple with children contacted my agent to view one of my properties I own. They loved the property, and it was an ideal home to bring up their children in. We agreed the rent and my agent set about doing the relevant reference and credit score checks. Despite the girlfriend of the couple having CCJs on her credit check, we agreed that if they paid a higher deposit and set up a standing order with the agency, we would happily take them.

I always feel people deserve a break and on paper they looked like ideal tenants. Both claimed to be working professionals and although I had never met them, my agent assured me that they were nice people.

I later discovered that they had both lied on their initial application and had provided false personal and work documents. Unfortunately, this had somehow got overlooked.

The couple moved in with their children and everything seemed fine for the first 12 months – although they were often late in paying their rent, but they claimed that they had changed banks and there were some confusions over setting up a new standing order.

Victorian houses are prone to damp due to their type of construction. They are prone to penetration from the rain and when the masonry gets very wet and doesn't have time to dry out, it eventually penetrates through to the internal walls. My tenants reported a problem with damp coming in from the bay window in one of the bedrooms, so we sent a damp specialist out to assess the situation.

The tenants, however, wouldn't allow the specialist into the property. We later discovered it was because they had brought three large dogs, a parrot and a few rabbits into the house without permission, despite there being a 'no pets' clause in the contract.

Because we couldn't access the building and the repair had not been seen to, the tenants decided to withhold their rent – for eight months. Claiming it was damaging their health (a classic old chestnut some tenants use because it's hard to prove otherwise). They also claimed they could only use one of the three bedrooms – this turned out to be another lie. Every time my agent tried to arrange an inspection or get a contractor in to look at the damp problem, they were met with a barrage of abuse from the male living there, who spat at and threatened anyone who walked up the path. When one of my contractors tried to attend to the problem from the outside of the house, the tenant shook his ladder, with the poor contractor standing at the top of it.

Despite my agent trying to reason with the couple, they continued to refuse access to the property or to pay their rent. We had no choice other than to issue a Section 21 notice to them to evict them from the property.

A Section 21 notice is a no-blame notice to vacate the property and gives the tenant two months' notice to leave the property by a fixed date. Again, the couple ignored the notice, so the next step was to issue a Section 8 notice, which states that court proceedings will be enforced if they don't leave.

They didn't leave – resulting in having to go to court to ask the judge for a court order to evict them. This took another two months. When we first went to court, the judge adjourned the case. The tenant's free legal advisor from the Citizens Advice Bureau, asked me if I would be willing to give the tenant another two months rent free to allow them to find another place to live. I declined on the grounds that they already owed me eight months' rent. The legal advisor then managed to persuade the judge to adjourn the case for two months so she could 'read the case notes'. A bit of a coincidence given that she had already asked me if I would give them two months extra time and I had said no.

In his defence notes, the tenant claimed that we had breached our contract by failing to have an annual gas safety inspection carried out on the property. Thankfully, our main gas contractor was prepared to testify that that tenant would not allow him into the property to do the inspection, despite three attempts.

The judge found in my favour and ordered the tenants to vacate the property within seven days, which they did. They did however write offensive messages and death threats all over the walls in the property before they left.

A year on and they still owe me eight months' rent, plus court fees, but I'm just thankful they have moved on. Having informed the police about the death threats, I later discovered that the tenants were already known to the police and had been arrested numerous times.

In addition to this, this was the same tenant who tried to get me into trouble with the ICO for sharing his information with the court.

A fellow landlord in America told me about his own experience of when discovering that his tenant was using his property as a drug drop-off, he tried to evict him only to have a gun pointed at his face and told in no uncertain terms that he would move out when he was good and ready and not before. He lost thousands of dollars in rent and was too afraid to inform the police, so he had to wait it out until the drug dealer decided to move on.

Unfortunately, every landlord will have a story to tell about a bad tenant and you soon realise it's an occupational hazard which is why it is so important to do thorough checks when you have someone interested in renting your property.

I don't want to put you off or make you think that no tenant can be trusted, because the majority of them are really lovely people and I have some super tenants. Just be aware that occasionally you may come across some who are awful.

NOTICES, EVICTIONS AND GOING TO COURT:

Guidelines for evicting a tenant from your property change quite frequently depending on how the government feel at any given time, but at the time of writing, these are the legal requirements for evicting a tenant.

Serving Notice:

As a landlord, you must give your tenant two months' notice

to vacate your property. You do this by serving them with a Section 21 document, which is commonly known as a 'no blame' eviction.

At the time of writing, the government are trying to have the Section 21 abolished. A Section 21 is a simple letter stating that you wish your tenant to move out by a certain date. Having brought up a family as a private renter for many years, I can understand why the government want to scrap the serving of the Section 21, because it's difficult for families with children to find suitable housing in the same area where their children go to school. However, I also feel it is also unfair to hold landlords to ransom by telling them who they can and can't have in the property which they, the landlord, pay the mortgage on.

A Section 21 will be served if for example you wish to sell your property, or live in it yourself, or your tenant has been difficult, missed, been late or withheld rent payments. You can only serve a section 21 once the tenant's fixed term AST has passed – usually six months.

You **MUST** serve the correct Section 21 form 6a, which is a 'no blame notice for repossession' notice. If you fail to do so, your notice will be void and you will have to re-serve it again. All notices can be found by visiting the National Residential Landlords Association website (NRLA).

Don't be tempted to serve any notice via email or other electronic means. Even if you received a 'read' report, it is difficult to prove in court that the recipient actually did read it themselves and a defence lawyer or judge will challenge it, which could push your eviction process back.

Sometimes a tenant will leave quietly, other times, you will have to take further action by serving a Section Eight notice.

Section Eight Notice:

If your tenant is responsible for rent arrears, involved in any criminal/antisocial behaviour, or has broken the terms of their tenancy agreement, you can serve them a Section Eight notice.

A Section Eight notice can be issued at any point in a tenancy, so you do not have to wait until the tenant's fixed term has ended. It is a more complicated form because you have to list why you wish the tenant to be evicted from the property. If the tenant is in arrears with their rent, they need to be in arrears by a minimum of two months.

Where the Section 21 gives the tenant two months' notice, the Section Eight gives a tenant just two weeks' notice to vacate the property. It also allows the landlord to apply to the courts to claim back the outstanding rent a tenant may owe.

When I took my tenants to court for withholding their rent, I was required to list the breaches of their tenancy, which included rent arrears of more than two months, antisocial behaviour, failure to allow contractors into the property and keeping pets without permission.

Serving a Section Eight must be done correctly, otherwise you will have to start the process all over again, so make sure you get it right first time. Again, all information about the correct way of serving any notice to your tenant can be found on the NRLA website and I urge any landlord to become a member because they have a whole legal team who can help you every step of the way. I am so thankful to the NRLA for their help with my first tenancy eviction. They talked me through every step of the process and even offered to represent me in court if I needed it.

You will need to provide evidence that you served your notice to your tenant – often they will claim that they didn't receive it. This can be hand-delivering it and videoing it on your phone with a time and date stamp, getting a witness to verify it was sent, or sending it by recorded delivery. The last option is a risky one because many tenants won't sign for recorded delivery. So, I would suggest you hand-deliver it and record the delivery on your phone or ask someone to be a witness for you.

Only when the two-week period is up can you then apply to the local magistrates' court to have your tenants evicted.

Unfortunately, some tenants are a step ahead of landlords and will have already been to a free advice centre who will tell them to stay where they are until the court date. Whilst no landlord wants to evict a tenant – after all, they pay the mortgage – in my opinion, it is wrong to advise tenants to wait until they are evicted by the court and made officially homeless, thus entitled to social housing. All this does is prolong things for everyone – and there is no escaping the fact that if a tenant owes rent, they will have to pay it eventually and they will have a County Court Judgement against them, which will make it incredibly difficult for them in the future.

Occasionally a tenant will go to their local authority after having been served a notice to quit with a story of how awful you are as a landlord to want to evict them. You are under no obligation to speak to the local authority or explain why you are evicting your tenant. Added to this, despite what some tenants think, someone in rent arrears is not automatically entitled to be rehoused by the local council if you serve them a section eight notice, because they would be considered to be voluntarily making themselves homeless by not paying their rent.

As a rule of thumb, always bear in mind that as nice as your tenants appear on paper or in person, people will and do become very different when they are faced with an eviction and will go to great lengths to stay in your property for as long as they can.

The Court Process:

Taking a tenant to court is not an ideal option, but sometimes a landlord has no other choice if a tenant is proving to be difficult. When I took my tenants to court, they owed eight months' rent and were adamant that they were going to stay in my property, rent free, for as long as possible, thanks to the advice given to them from a housing charity. For those eight months I still had to pay the mortgage.

Mortgage companies are not interested if a tenant refuses to pay their rent; they still want you to pay your mortgage payments. Thankfully I have other properties that can make up the shortfall and I also work full time as a writer, so although it was a loss that I will never recover, I could manage to still make the payments, but this is not always the case, particularly if you only have one or two properties.

When taking a tenant to court for repossession for your property, you need to make sure that the forms you fill out are a) the right forms and b) filled out correctly. I made the mistake of not signing one form and the court sent them back, thus delaying the whole process for another week.

The NRLA (National Residential Landlords Association) are always on hand to help you fill the correct forms out and they were invaluable to me when it came to explaining what would happen in court, so I would advise you become a member. For around £10/month it's well worth it.

Your paperwork will consist of a form for possession of your property and you will have to outline the reasons why you feel the judge should award in your favour. You will also be asked to supply a statement of events leading up to your request for eviction. A copy of these will be sent to the tenant and they will have the opportunity to say why they feel they are entitled to remain as a tenant in your property.

Unfortunately, it does cost you to take your tenant to court – around £350, depending on where you live, but you can apply to reclaim these costs after the hearing, although, again, this will cost and for most landlords, they are just relieved to have their property back.

Once you have filed your paperwork with your local magistrate court and it's all been checked, you will be sent a court date. Don't assume for one minute that you will gain possession of your property by this date.

When my court date came up, the judge hadn't had time to read through the tenant's statement and at the same time, the tenant's free legal advisor had managed to persuade the judge to defer the court date, allowing the tenant to stay in my property for another two months.

You really do have to try and not take it personally when you are faced with a tenant refusing to leave your property. The British legal system is often a law unto themselves and they are supposed to take an unbiased view on the situation, although I have found this is not always the case.

When you do attend court, always dress smart and act professionally. It shouldn't matter how you dress, but it does help if you go into court as a professional, rather than going in there looking for a fight with your tenant.

Going to court can feel quite intimidating, particularly when you may come face to face with an angry tenant justifying their case. All courts have security to ensure that should any trouble start they can step in and you will not usually have to sit near your tenant while you wait for your case to be called. Again, treat it as business. Emotions may be running high and your tenant may be ready for a fight, but don't be tempted to retaliate either inside or outside of the court room.

The court process should only take around half an hour, if the judge has read all the statements presented to him/her. It's a rather informal meeting consisting of you, the tenant (if they turn up), an usher and any witnesses. In my court case, it was the judge, me and two people from my agency. The tenant didn't turn up for the final hearing, which I think helped to go in my favour. If you can't be bothered to turn up to your court hearing, you can't be that concerned to keep a roof over your head.

Out of respect answer any questions from the judge with 'Sir', 'Madam', or 'Your Honour' and always keep to the facts. The judge is not interested in any hearsay of 'he said-she said'.

Everything that needs to be said should be in your statement.

The judge will ask you how much rent your tenant owes you, or why you are seeking an order of possession. He/she will also ask if you wish to reclaim the money you are owed if you are awarded a possession order.

The judge will then decide on whether you have a reasonable case for repossession and if so, will allow the tenant seven days in which to leave the property. He/she will also instruct the tenant to pay your arrears and court costs.

Unfortunately, if the tenant isn't compliant and doesn't leave your property, you then have to reapply to the court (another cost) to instruct the bailiffs to evict your tenant. Also, if your tenant doesn't pay you your arrears, you then have to apply again to the court to enforce repayment and this will cost you again.

It's a very unfair system, which is why it is so important to do your checks before you allow a tenant into your property.

As a word of warning, don't be tempted to employ a debt recovery agency yourself to get your money back! I made the mistake of paying £950 to a company to recover the money owed to me and two years later they have still failed to do so, despite knowing the tenant is still living locally. My only other option now is to pay for a court order to issue a CCJ, which will cost another £450, but I'm just happy that they no longer live in my house.

Another word of warning – if you are using an agent, once the Section 21/Section Eight notice has been filed and the notice to quit date has passed, many will have nothing more to do with the case and it will be up to you to take the next steps on your own. This is where places like the NRLA help. I feel it's very unfair for an agent to just drop a landlord when they realise they will not be getting paid their commission once the landlord has filed for eviction.

I was lucky in that two people from the agency I used offered to come to court with me, but this isn't always the case with many agents. After all, they've done their job and won't get paid any further commission, so why would they help you out? It is a business.

I really hope you don't have to go through a repossession process, but if you do, just remember, you are one of many landlords fighting to reclaim your property and there is a lot of help out there if you need it. You are not alone.

Unfortunately, at the moment, rent arrears do not show up on credit reports unless you apply to the court for a County Court Judgement against your tenants. You are able to refuse to provide a reference to future landlords and if the matter has gone to court, you are allowed to say why you refuse because it is a public record that anyone can look up.

Recovering Costs:

For an additional fee, some agents offer a rent guarantee scheme so that if your tenant doesn't pay their rent, they will ensure you still get your money. However, make sure you read the contract before paying and signing it. Many will only offer two months' worth of rent cover. So, if you are unable to evict your tenant for six months because you are taking them to court, you will still lose four months' worth of rent. There are landlord insurance companies that offer the same service, a lot cheaper, but again, double check exactly what they are offering you and how long they will pay your rent for. Very few have an open guarantee policy.

A Debt Collection Service:

I'm personally against employing debt collection services to collect rent arrears, due to a bad experience with using one. Having paid £950 to a debt collection service to recover rent arrears for me, the company who claim on their website to be 'the best in the business', simply took my money and did nothing to recover the debt.

Clients were told to log into the company's portal to see progress of their case. Every entry was a single line stating they had called/emailed the client. No transcript or evidence that they did this, and their contract stipulates (in the tiniest of writing) that the fee is non-refundable.

Even when I supplied them with my tenant's new address, they did nothing to chase the money they still owed me. Eighteen months later and I am still waiting. Many of these debt recovery companies are charlatans who take your money and do nothing to recover the debt. And please do not be tempted to take up any offer from someone who will 'sort it' for you. You could end up back in court on a charge of harassment from your tenant. As tempting as it is to get revenge, it really isn't worth it. If you need to recover money from a tenant, do it through the correct channels. In my experience, people who abuse the system tend to get their comeuppance eventually.

When you get repossession of your property:

The first thing to do when you do get possession of your property is to change the locks. Even if you have had to have bailiffs in to break down the door to evict the tenant, you will be responsible for changing the locks.

The reason I advise you to change the locks is because you don't know who might have a copy, and the last thing you need is a vengeful tenant returning in the middle of the night to destroy your property.

THE IMPORTANCE OF A CONTINGENCY PLAN:

It's really important to have a contingency plan in hand because I can guarantee you one thing – nothing ever goes to plan when you are a property investor!

As we've seen above, there will be times when your tenants might not pay their rent on time, or even stop paying altogether.

You will however still be responsible for paying the mortgage on your property and if you don't have any other income coming in, it can prove difficult to persuade your mortgage lender to help you out.

There will be times when a boiler needs replacing. Your EPC certificate might have run out. You have to have your annual gas safety inspection carried out every year by law. Even something as simple as a toilet not flushing or a leaky pipe will have to be repaired at your cost, so it pays to make sure you have a 'repairs account' with some money set aside for when these things happen – and believe me, they will happen.

Even if you have landlord's insurance, you don't really want to make a claim for something simple such as a leaky tap because invariably your premiums will increase every time you make a claim. Save your insurance claim for when something big happens, as in the case of a tractor and a car driving through the fence of one of my properties in the same weekend, causing thousands pounds worth of damage!

The length of time it can often take between tenants moving out and another moving in can be anything from a couple of weeks to a couple of months, depending on how much notice the new tenant has to give their landlord. Or you might be without a tenant for six months because you haven't been able to find someone suitable. Can you still pay the mortgage if this happens?

2020 was hit with the biggest pandemic of our time and left a lot of people without a job, resulting in many unable to pay their rent. Whilst mortgage companies gave landlords payment holidays, the payments were still added to the mortgage. If you are reliant solely on your income from property investment, you do need to have something you can fall back on if and when things like this happen.

With the number of properties I own, not a month has gone by without having to pay for something on at least one property. It might be something as simple as a blown fuse or, as recently happened, my tenant left a tap on in the bathroom for the weekend, resulting in the ceiling falling down – thankfully, the insurance company covered the costs.

CHECK LIST FOR ALL LANDLORDS:

Whether you use an agent, or you are self-managing your property, as a landlord, you MUST provide your tenant by law with the following prior to them moving into your property:

- A signed AST
- A copy of Fair Processing Notice (you can download a copy from www.gov.uk)
- A copy of the How to Rent (you can download a copy from www.gov.uk)
- An up to date EPC certificate (go to www.epcregister.com to check that your property has one.)
- An up to date copy of your Gas Safety Inspection.
- A copy of your electrical certificate (law for all new tenancies a/o 2020)
- A copy of the Tenancy Deposit Certificate

A WORD ABOUT TAX:

My accountant once told me; income is income. Regardless of whether you own one property, or you have multiple properties generating enough income for you never to have to work again, you are responsible for declaring any income you receive. As I'm not a tax expert or an accountant, I won't go into tax issues, but unless you are good at filling out self-assessments and feel confident to do your own, it's advisable to employ an accountant to do this for you.

As with hiring anyone to deal with your business, always find out as much as you can before hiring someone to deal with your money on your behalf. Again, personal recommendation is always the best policy, but also do your own checks on how long someone has been trading, do they had any complaints registered against them? Are they experts in property accounts? There are many accountancy firms that specialise in property investment and tax laws, so spend a bit of time researching them before committing yourself to one.

Always keep receipts of anything that has been bought for your business. This can be materials, invoices for labour, office equipment, even stamps to send your accounts off to your accountant. Your accountant will tell you if you can or can't include an expense.

There is also a lot of information on the HMRC website about tax for the self-employed.

A WORD ABOUT ACCOUNTANTS:

Whilst my accountant is an absolute angel and always has my best interests at heart, there are some who are either not experienced in property accounts or are just dishonest. It's vital that you find an accountant who you can trust.

In the UK there are several qualifications that an accountant can hold, including:

- Chartered Tax Advisor – CTA, ATII or FTII – Member or Fellow of the Chartered Institute of Taxation (CIOT)
- Chartered Certified Accountant – ACCA or FCCA – Member or Fellow or the Association of Chartered Certified Accountants (ACCA)
- Chartered Accountant – ACA or FCA – Member or Fellow of the Institute of Chartered Accountants in England and Wales (ICAEW)
- Chartered Accountant – CA – Member of the Institute of Chartered Accountants in Scotland (ICAS)
- Chartered Accountant – ACA or FCA – Member or Fellow of Chartered Accountants Ireland (formally, but still

legally known as the Institute of Chartered Accountants Ireland (ICAI)) (CAI)

- Chartered Management Accountant – ACMA or FCMA – Member or Fellow of the Chartered Institute of Management Accountants (CIMA)
- Certified Public Accountant – ASPA or FSPA – Associate or Fellow of the Association of Certified Public Accountants (ACPA)

Don't be tempted to hire a general bookkeeper to oversee your accounts. You might be able to manage your self-assessment for your income and outgoings for a single property, but there are many tax legalities around property income that you won't be familiar with, but a property accountant will.

If you discover your accountant has been dishonest you can ask the Financial Ombudsman Service to investigate.

SECTION TWO
YOUR PROPERTY NEEDS RENOVATING

This section of the book is dedicated to those properties that require attention prior to being let out. Whether you have bought a cheap property at auction or discovered the real reason your property was so cheap was because the roof is about to fall down.

Whilst I am not a trained builder, I have spent several years on site, learning on the job from various contractors and have had my fair share of cowboys to deal with, so I am writing this from my own experiences so that hopefully you will be fully aware of what is involved in the process of renovating a property.

Neglected Properties:

Oftentimes you will come across a property that has been on the market for some time and has been neglected. These are sometimes properties of the deceased and will be part of their estate. Whilst as a buyer you can often get a good deal with such a property, it will be sold 'as seen' because the family just want to sell it. Similar properties are those where an elderly person has moved into a retirement home or in with family and they wish to sell their house.

Whilst I wouldn't necessarily recommend a first-time investor start out with such a property, there is a certain feeling of achievement when you complete a renovation like this and restore a property to a more modern standard.

You solicitor and valuer are paid to check that a property is of saleable standards and to check that building regs have been adhered to, should there be any alterations to a property, but it always pays to have a surveyor check an older property to make sure there are no signs of damp, subsidence or major cracks you need to be worried about.

It's also a good idea to take a professional builder along with you prior to buying a property that needs some restoration. A good builder can spot if there are any major problems with a building and advise whether it's a good investment or it's going to cost a fortune to restore.

Advisory Improvements:

I've bought many older properties that have the bathroom downstairs and whilst it's tempting to move it upstairs, I've found that tenants don't seem to mind having their bathroom on the ground floor.

Moving a bathroom upstairs can be a relatively easy job, but unless you want to start extending pipes all over the property, you can be somewhat limited as to where to place a new bathroom, so I'd advise if you buy a property with a downstairs bathroom, to just leave it where it is. After all, you won't be living in it, and a tenant will see it is downstairs before signing a rental contract.

It pays to update a bathroom if it requires it. Bathrooms and kitchens always add value to a property, as does a loft room, conservatory, additional bedrooms, a cloak room, an ensuite and a garage.

If your property has no off-street parking, but you can drop the kerb and add a private drive, it will not only appeal more to tenants, it will add to the value of the property. A loft room adds around £12,000 to a property, so whilst it is an expensive option, it does make sense if you have enough headroom space and landing space to create another room upstairs.

Kitchens and Bathrooms:

People use these spaces every single day so it's worth updating an old/tired kitchen and bathroom in any renovation project. There are two ways you can do this: the first is to employ a contractor who specialises in fitting kitchens and bathrooms.

They will buy, supply, and fit everything necessary, so you don't have to lift a finger.

Whilst there are many good contractors out there, there are equally many who are not as honest as you would expect. I've had fitters who have bought very basic kitchen and bathroom appliances and charged me an absolute fortune for them, plus more for fitting them.

There are many DIY stores that provide everything from design to supply and fitting and if you are looking at having someone provide this sort of service, this is the best option because you will always have a guarantee of work and materials from the store should anything go wrong.

Do be aware though that many DIY stores employ local builders and contractors to carry out their work orders, so whilst you will be covered by the store's guarantee, you may still be dealing with Bob the Builder from down the road, who may not have the best reputation.

Another option is to buy the materials such as the bath, sink, WC, kitchen worktops, etc yourself and hire a builder/fitter to fit them. Whilst this is a much cheaper option and there won't be any hidden mark-up on materials, please do your homework on hiring a professional tradesperson.

I would advise you to stay clear from websites that promise a professional tradesperson via their website. In the UK there are no specific accredited associations that tradespeople have to adhere to, so anyone can claim they are a builder, plumber, etc. These websites are nothing more than advertising agencies for tradespeople, charging them an annual membership to advertise through them.

In the early days, I made the mistake of thinking that if I used a builder recommended by a trade website, I would at least have some guarantee that the work would be of a high standard. It was not. The work had to be redone, costing me more money with no recompense from the previous builder or the company who recommended him.

The best way to find a good, honest, and reliable tradesperson is by word of mouth recommendation. Although there are no guarantees to who you will end up with and how good they will be, it is the best way to find someone for the job because you can see other work that they might have done for friends or neighbours, etc.

Again, when you find someone you think might be a good fit for your work, do as much research as you can into that person. Look for them on social media. If they are a limited company, put in their company name into the Companies House Register to see how long they have been trading. Have they had any other companies in other names? Sometimes tradesmen go bankrupt and start another company in another name. Look up review sites such as Trust Pilot to see if they have any work reviews. Don't just accept their quote because it's cheap and always get at least three different quotes for any work.

Another sign of a good tradesperson is that they can't fit your job in for a few weeks. If a tradesperson is busy, it means they have regular work.

It's really important to check qualifications if you are employing an electrician, a plumber, or a gas engineer. These tradespeople have to be qualified, but you'll be amazed at how many claim they are and they're not. A builder I hired some years ago told me that his cousin was an electrician and would sort out the wiring for a new kitchen I was having fitted. It turned out he barely knew how to change a plug, let alone do all the electrics in my kitchen – in fact, I think I knew more about electrics than he did!

I'm very much in favour of what I call the 'old-school' tradesperson. This is someone who has been in the building business for many years and is either semi-retired or has a few regular customers he works for. In my time renovating properties, it's the old-school tradesman who will get the job done at a reasonable price and they won't be tempted to rip you off, because it's just not the done thing as far as they're concerned.

Alternatively, if you're feeling brave, you can buy and fit your own kitchen and bathroom. Many kitchen and bathroom suppliers will design your space free of charge when you buy their products, so if you have a bit of experience with building or feel like having a go, you can do it yourself. There are many good videos on YouTube that will take you through every step of fitting a new bathroom or a kitchen.

Because it will be a rental property, don't go too expensive with your designs and fittings. Do make sure that your appliances and fittings are going to be able to stand a fair amount of wear and tear and as tempting as it is to put in a jacuzzi bath tub and hand stencil the walls, you are not going to be living in the property, so don't waste your money on extras.

Windows and Doors:

Windows and doors are obviously needed in any property. Building Regulations state that certain standards must be met when a window or door is replaced. It has been a legal requirement since April 2012 for all uPVC window installations in the UK to be fully compliant with current Building Regulations.

You will have already checked that your property has working doors and windows, but if any need replacing, whilst it is quite a simple job to do, it will pay to have them replaced by a professional window/door fitter and not just a general contractor. If you decide to fit them yourself or get someone other than a professional window fitter to do them, you still have to comply with Building Regulations.

Whilst there is no specific law to state that your current windows must have trickle vents (a small flap that allows air to flow into a room), they do state that if you are replacing a window with a trickle vent, you do need to replace it with one that has a trickle vent.

Rooms such as bathrooms and kitchens are notorious for getting damp problems caused by condensation because they don't get enough ventilation and steam from cooking or hot water settles on the walls. Whilst it's easy enough to open the windows on a daily basis, many tenants don't do this. If you have trickle vents in place it helps to keep these areas in a property dry. It's fairly easy to install a trickle vent in a window that doesn't currently have one and costs a lot less than installing a new window.

Older properties often have single-glazed, wooden framed windows. If you are renting your property out, windows have to be double-glazed and FENSA approved. FENSA is a governmental authorised scheme that guarantees new windows and fitting comply with the Building Standards Regulations. All UK window fitters have to be FENSA approved and will carry a certificate to this effect.

As with windows, doors have to be compliant with Building Standards Regulations and Energy Efficiency Regulations. According to the Building Regulations Planning Portal, doors must comply with thermal heat loss regulations, have safety glass, be fire retardant and have means of ventilation – for example to allow steam from a bathroom/kitchen to escape. You can find out more about regulations for windows and doors by going to: https://www.planningportal.co.uk/info/200130/common_projects/14/doors_and_windows/2

Flooring:

When you buy an older property you will often find that the flooring has been down for years and once you rip up that lime green, 1970's floral carpet there could be unknown problems with the floorboards that may have been down since the property was first built.

The worst-case scenario with original flooring is that it might be riddled with dry rot or an infestation of wood termites and you will need to replace it all. Most often you might find a few loose floorboards or some with a slight bit of damage. Always check under the carpets of an older property – you don't want a tenant falling through your ceiling because they've stood on a rotten floorboard.

When replacing flooring in a rental property, consider that it needs to be hard wearing, so if you are going to have carpets in the bedrooms and landing, make sure you get a good quality, hard wearing product and thick underlay. It's very tempting to have bare floorboards in a property, but you do have to make sure that all nails are countersunk and that the wood has been sanded and treated and that any gaps between the boards are filled in with a clear filler. Otherwise your tenants are going to complain about cut or cold feet.

For living areas where you get a lot of traffic, such as the lounge, dining room, bathrooms, hallways, and kitchens, it's a good idea to have hardwood laminated flooring laid down. Vinyl flooring is ideal for bathrooms and kitchens, but again, get a good quality range because it can easily tear or chip when furniture/white goods is moved around.

Budget:

I always tell people who are investing in a property and thinking of modernising a building, to have a budget and to stick to it. Whilst buying a property to renovate sounds like an ideal opportunity to put your stamp on it, costs soon mount up when it comes to getting it to suitable rental standards. Even though you can save a lot of costs by doing the decorating and painting yourself, you will at some point need to get a professional in for fitting kitchens and bathrooms, etc unless you are experienced in doing this.

Decoration:

When it comes to decorating your property for the rental market, keep it simple and clean. If you start adding wallpaper feature walls in rooms and the paper gets ripped, you will have to re-paper the area and you might not be able to find the same batch.

Most landlords paint their properties in white or magnolia trade paint which is quite hardwearing and easy to freshen up once a tenant leaves.

When I first started out in rental properties, I would put artwork up on the walls and leave vases of dried flowers and candles on mantle pieces. I've even bought ornaments and rugs for the properties. It was only when a tenant called to ask if I could pick up the artwork I'd left on the walls when he moved in because he didn't like it, that I realised our tastes differ and what I would have in my home, isn't necessarily what a tenant would choose.

Tenants want a blank canvas when they move into a property, so always bear this in mind when you're decorating. It's fine to add decorative features for the staging purposes for photographs and viewings, but remove them once you've found a tenant.

You do need to make sure that curtain/blind fittings are in place too. Most landlords put up standard curtain poles and curtain rings on each window. Some include curtains, but again, our tastes differ, and many tenants bring their own window dressings with them or buy new and take them with them when they leave.

Gardens:

Gardens need to be secured with fencing or walls so that if a tenant has pets or small children they are not going to escape. You are not obliged to maintain a tenant's garden once they move into your property, nor do you need to buy any gardening equipment – that is the responsibility of the tenant.

You do, however, have to make sure that any garden areas are safe from trip or slip hazards. It's always a good idea to get an outside tap installed when you are renovating a property too.

I've always allowed my tenants to do what they like with their gardens including putting up sheds, workshops, and garden features. As long as they don't put in a permanent structure such as a conservatory, I'm quite happy for them to do what they want to make the outdoor areas their own.

Conservatories:

The property you have bought might have enough space to add a conservatory to it. According to the latest building regulations, conservatories fall into the category of the 'permitted development scheme' which basically means you are allowed to erect a conservatory and do not usually require planning permission from your local authority. One reason you will require permission is if your property is a listed building or is likely to cause concern to your neighbours.

Depending on your local authority, you may have to seek permission if your conservatory adds over 100 sq metres of floor space. Conservatories are classed as an extension to a property and although you don't necessarily have to apply for planning permission, you are still required to adhere to extension rules and regulations.

Extension Regs:

With any extension to a property, only half of the area around the original footprint of the house can be covered with any extension, including a conservatory and they are not allowed to be higher than the apex of the original roof, including the height of the original eaves.

An extension cannot be built without planning permission at the front of a property or on the side if the side looks onto a highway. Side-extensions to a house must be single storey and can only be up to half the width of the original house to get away without planning permission.

Single-storey rear extensions cannot extend beyond the rear wall of the original house by more than four metres if a detached house, or more than three metres for any other house.

Extensions of more than one storey must not extend beyond the rear wall of the original house by more than three metres or be within seven metres of any boundary opposite the rear wall of the house.

The roof pitch must match existing house as far as practicable and any upper-floor window located in a 'side elevation' must be obscure-glazed.

All side extensions of more than one storey will require householder planning permission.

Extensions, whether a conservatory or a permanent brick building, will certainly add value to your property and can turn a two-up-two-down into a three- or four-bedroom house which will give you a greater rental return.

Again, as I keep pointing out, do your homework when deciding on employing someone to build a conservatory or extension on your property and make sure you check with your local authority that you don't require planning permission because they can ask you to remove it if you haven't applied when you should have.

Loft Extensions:

Planning permission is not usually required for a loft extension because you are not directly adding space to your property. The space is already there, and you are using it for a different purpose. However, you must meet certain guidelines to carry out a loft extension:

The total area of the additional space won't exceed 40 cubic metres for terraced houses or 50 cubic metres for detached or semi-detached houses (this allowance includes not only any extra space you create with this loft, but also any previous additions that have been made, such as an extension)

- The extension does not reach beyond the outermost part of the existing roof slope at the front of the house.
- The extension does not go higher than the highest part of the roof.
- Materials are similar in appearance to the existing house.
- There are no verandas, balconies or raised platforms.
- Side-facing windows are obscure-glazed (frosted or patterned to stop people seeing in). Side-facing window openings are 1.7m or more above the floor.
- Your house is not on designated land, namely national parks, areas of Outstanding National Beauty, the Broads, conservation areas and World Heritage sites.
- Roof extensions, other than hip-to-gable ones, are set back as far as practicable, at least 20cm from the original eaves.
- The roof enlargement does not overhang the outer face of the wall of the original house.

Always ask a builder or your local authority to check that your proposed loft extension meets these requirements.

With any loft extension you do need to adhere to building regulations, which include:

- Any work done is structurally sound.
- That the new room is fire safe and that sound is reasonably insulated between the loft and the rooms below.
- Fire-resistant doors will be needed to make the new room fire safe.
- Mains-powered smoke alarms need to be fitted.
- New floor joists will be needed to support the weight of the new room.

- Sound insulation: it's important to make sure that noise between rooms is sufficiently insulated.
- A new staircase will be needed to provide escape in the event of a fire (retractable staircases and ladders aren't enough).
- Any new walls will need to support any existing or new roofs where existing supports have been removed.

Additional building regulations to any extension include:

- **Party Wall Agreement:** If the work you're planning is going to affect the wall that joins your house to your neighbour's, you'll need to have a Party Wall Agreement. This is an agreement between you and your neighbour that aims to ensure that work done is fair and won't endanger your neighbour's property. You'll need to give a Party Wall Notice – a summary of your proposed work and copies of your plans – to your adjoining neighbours. You can find free templates for these online or get help from your builder or architect. It's then up to your neighbour to sign their agreement. If they are concerned, they may request an independent party wall surveyor to approve the work. You can recommend a surveyor, but it's ultimately up to them to decide who they use, and you're obliged to pay for their services. The surveyor will come and inspect the plans, and may request further documentation, before signing off the work to go ahead, or asking for any reasonable amendments to be made. You can find out more about the Party Wall etc Act 1966 and what it covers by visiting the government planning website.

- **Protected Species:** If you think you have bats living in your loft, you'll need to have a bat survey, which can cost

£300 to £400. Bats are a protected species and, if your loft is home to a roost of them, you may need to obtain a mitigation licence to carry out the work.

*Source – Which.co.uk

BIGGER PROJECTS:

Sometimes you will find a very cheap property which looks like it would be an ideal rental, but not in its current state and will need a major renovation.

In 2014 I found such a property purely by chance. I was originally interested in a property just up the road from this one and was all set to complete on it, when my solicitor discovered that because it was originally a post office, it required a commercial mortgage on it, rather than a BTL mortgage. My lender wasn't keen and unfortunately, I had to pull out of the sale.

However, I noticed that a few doors up, there was another property for sale. It was a two-up-two-down purple cottage. The couple who owned it had separated and they had to sell it quickly to pay off their outstanding mortgage.

There was nothing pretty about this cottage and it was falling apart, but I knew it had potential, so I offered the amount they were asking and set about working out how I could return it to a lovely home.

A local architect who had previously done some work for me drew up some plans to turn it into a four-bedroom house and I got together a team of local tradesmen to help me renovate it.

If you are ever thinking of taking on a big project like this, you will need to get planning permission for a change of property along with adhering to building regulations. Don't assume that you can pull an existing property down without asking permission.

This project took 14 months and I had a lot of unexpected problems along the way: the roof joists were so old that they were dangerous, so we had to put a whole new roof on – an unexpected cost of £10,000. The village the cottage was in was prone to bats, so I had to pay for the local environmental group to check that there were no bats or nests up there.

The property was showing signs of subsidence at the back and upon closer inspection by a structural engineer, we were told that end of the house had to be demolished and new footings installed, which meant digging down three metres and laying a mental grid in the ground to support the property – another cost of £10,000.

Because the original property was built in the 1600s, the stonework was crumbling away, so we had to knock down almost every wall and rebuild it. It would have been cheaper to demolish the whole lot, but planning had told us that we had to keep 10% of the original property, so we literally kept one external wall that housed the chimney.

Additional costs incurred, such as having to have traffic lights installed when we wanted to paint the side of the house which was adjacent to the main road.

Because we were a small team, I spent every day working on the property. During that time, I learned everything there was to learn about building a property from scratch. From learning how to safely remove a roof to operating a mini-digger and installing a kitchen.

As hard and frustrating it was at times, aside from having my children, it has to be one of the best experiences of my life and such a feeling of accomplishment when we finally finished and christened it with a bottle of champagne.

Today the property is valued at three times what I paid for it and is one of my best rentals and although I've had to have some maintenance work done on it, due to some of my contractors cutting corners, the purple cottage is now a beautiful cream, four-bed house with a study, hi-tech kitchen and three bathrooms and has been home to a wonderful family.

Workforce:

When you take on a big renovation project such as the one I did above, you need to make sure your staff are reliable, honest and have a good work ethic, but this is not always easy.

Being a woman, working in a primarily male dominated trade had many challenges and I can't tell you the amount of times I was treated with utter contempt by men in the industry. From being laughed at in builders' merchants to being taken advantage of from those who worked for me. Being blonde and only five foot tall, didn't help matters either! And whilst you would hope that people were more open to women working in predominantly male roles, building is still a very male-dominated profession and it takes a lot of energy to get people to take you seriously and know that you mean business.

Whilst about 70% of the time my team were good at what they did, there were times when, if I wasn't on site, they wouldn't do any work. Being the project manager of a build means you will encounter problems, whether it's staff not turning up on time or when they do, they have no intention of putting in a full days' work. A builder I hired could only ever manage a three-day week because he was either ill or hungover and often wouldn't arrive on site until 10.30am and finish by 2.30pm, but still expected to be paid a full-time wage.

A plasterer I hired refused to put a mix on after midday, claiming it wouldn't have time to dry out. I employed a plumber who broke a brand new £600 boiler by knocking his coffee down the back of it when he and his mate were playing football. I've had to have a property completely re-wired after an electrician had wired everything up wrong and then disappeared.

I've had a roofing contractor turn up to repair the roof as high as a kite. I discovered one of my builders had stolen thousands of pounds from my budget to fund his drug habit. A bathroom fitter charged me twice for a bathroom suite. I've had a painter spill a pot of white glass all over a brand-new carpet and leave it to dry over the weekend. A kitchen fitter charged me for a brand new cooker, only to later discover that it was an old one from another job he'd worked on. A tiler stuck broken tiles on a bathroom wall, and I've had a few contractors walk out in the middle of a job, never to be seen again.

Every landlord learns the hard way and there are many worse horror stories than mine out there. If I was to take every cowboy builder I've had to deal with to the small claims court I wouldn't get anything else done. Unfortunately, sometimes you have to put it down to experience.

I decided in future to never hire sole traders and only hire from a reputable local building company who I have since worked with for the past few years. They guarantee every job, I don't ever pay in advance and until I'm happy with the work and they have a large team of professional and experienced men and women who have been with the company for many years.

Check List for Hiring Tradespeople:

Whether you are doing a small or large property renovation, it pays to check and double check who you're dealing with. With my past experiences of working with tradespeople I have made a list to go through, so that you hopefully won't have to experience what I've experienced over the years:

Always ask for at least three references from previous customers – an honest tradesperson will be happy and proud to refer you to work they have previously done.

Always check a person's social media – this will tell you what sort of person you are dealing with.

Never pay upfront for materials or labour – a professional contractor will have trade accounts with builder's merchants/ kitchen and bathroom suppliers/paint shops, etc.

Never divulge your budget or allow someone else to be in charge of your budget.

- Ask for receipts for everything – the amount of times I have paid full price for materials, only to find out that they are sub-standard.
- Never pay for labour upfront – always check the quality of work prior to paying anything.
- Check a person's qualifications – being able to change a plug and being a qualified electrician are two very different things.
- Be friendly, but do not assume your workforce are your best mates – they are being paid to do a job and you are just another customer to them. Even if you are working with them on a big project, keep them outside of your circle of friends.
- If you are doing a large renovation, stick to a budget for materials and labour. Don't be tempted into paying wages in advance or lending money to your workforce, however much they plead.
- Keep boundaries – if you feel someone is overstepping the mark by being constantly late or doing substandard work, tell them and get rid of them.
- Ensure that you are all singing from the same worksheet – explain the job, the timescale you need it done by and how much you have agreed to pay for the work to be completed.
- Never pay a builder in cash – even if they tell you it will be cheaper. You have no record of paying them. Always stick to cheque or bank transfer.
- Should you be unfortunate enough to discover you have hired a rogue builder, contact Citizens Advice and report them to Trading Standards and the Office of Fair Trading. If your builder asks for payment in cash, it usually means he does not declare his earnings. Inform HMRC of his name and address. Unfortunately, we still have no governing body that builders are accountable to, so

anyone can say they are a general builder. Thankfully, we do have a legal system, so if you suffer at the hands of a cowboy builder, you still have the option of going through the small claims court.

• Always get estimates in writing and if you are having a big job done such as an extension or a big renovation project, have a contract of works drawn up and signed by both parties.

Whilst it's inevitable that you will run into problems throughout your career as a property investor, the positives do outweigh the negatives.

As in life, you will come into contact with people who will try to harm your business through jealousy, greed or just because they're not very nice people. The amount of times I've been told I'm so lucky to be in the position I'm in! And yes, part of it is luck, but 99% of doing anything successful is putting in the hard work and taking the risks that others aren't prepared to take and to keep chipping away at it.

Don't let the naysayers in your life influence you. Just keep on following the advice of people who have already done what you want to do. Not everything is going to work in the same way. You might initially struggle to find a lender, but don't stop chasing your dream – there are many lenders out there who would be only too happy to lend to you. There will be times when contractors let you down, deadlines will be missed, and you will question whether it really was worth all the time, money, and energy. Yes, it is. Don't be put off when things don't quite go to plan.

You'll often lose out on what might seem to be the perfect rental, but there will always be properties to buy and there will be another perfect rental out there for you and you will always come across contractors who think short-term and will try to get as much out of you for a job as they can, but there will also be honest and reliable ones who will stick by you for the long-term.

And there will always be tenants who will ruin your property and fail to pay their rent, but there will also be tenants who will stay with you for years and who you will build up good relations with. Don't be put off from one or two bad experiences.

Chapter Six

Where Do We Go From Here?

Once you have one BTL property you will be well on your way to start adding to your portfolio. At the time of writing, half of all UK property investors own one BTL property. 30% own between one and three properties. The other 20% have grown their portfolios and have more than six rental properties.

If you are serious about investing in property and making a career out of becoming a landlord, I always advise of the dangers in having just one property. Having just one property limits you. You are more likely to have to continue to work if you only have one property because there will be times when, whilst the rent will cover your mortgage payments, it may not cover other expenses such as a new boiler or maintenance repairs. Added to this, if your tenant leaves, or fails to pay their rent for a period of time, if you have no other income coming in, you still have to find a way to pay for the mortgage on the property.

As with anything in life, the more you do it, the easier it becomes and once you've bought your first investment property, you will already have experienced what it's like to work with estate agents, solicitors, mortgage lenders and tenants and will hopefully be prepared for any legalities that come with being a landlord.

Generating Income for your Second BTL Property:

In simple terms, when you purchased your first BTL property, you would have paid a deposit (usually around 25% of the value of the property). This means that the property you bought is already worth more than the money you owe on it, which in turn means that you will usually be able to ask your lender if you can take that amount (the amount you paid as a deposit) out of the value of your property to pay the deposit and legal fees on a second property.

So, for example, if your first property cost £150,000, you would have paid £37,500 as the deposit, so you will actually only owe your mortgage lender £112,500 on that property. If you wanted to release some money out of that first property to fund the deposit on a second property, you would need to get your property valued. Depending on the country's economic climate at the time, your property may well have increased in value. If, for example, your £150,000 property is now valued at £175,000, it means that, depending on your lender's LTV (loan to value criteria) you could potentially have £63,000 available for you to invest in a second or even a third BTL property.

At the very least (as long as your property hasn't decreased in value) you would have your initial deposit available to use as your next deposit. Depending on a lender's LTV (loan to value) criteria, will depend on how much equity they will allow you to release. This could be 70 – 80% of the current value of your property.

Typically, you need to own a property for six months before you can borrow the equity out of it. This is to prevent money laundering. Having said that there are some lenders who will have 'day one' re-mortgages. For example, if you find an auction property you wish to by next, these have to be planned in advance with your lender, so that you are ready to buy at an auction.

You don't have to stick with your first lender either. There are plenty of lenders who will happily look at your current mortgage and assess whether or not your property has increased in value and if you can pull some money out of it to use as a deposit for property number two.

They will want to make sure that you have kept up to date with your repayments and that your rental income more than covers your mortgage on a property.

Some lenders allow what is known as top slicing. This is where they assess your own disposable income/other earnings and allow you to subsidise the rent with it in order to afford a higher affordability.

Most property landlords have their mortgages on a BTL (Buy-to-Let), interest only basis – meaning that you only pay the interest back monthly and hope that your property doesn't decrease in value when the time comes to repay the mortgage (usually 25 years).

It's very rare that a property decreases in value. Even if the country suffers an economic recession, economists say that it does recover quite quickly, so by the time you come to sell your property, it should still hold its value and hopefully will have increased significantly in value.

It is however up to you whether you chose an interest only mortgage. You have the option to have a capital repayment mortgage, which will pay more off the original mortgage and often you can pay an extra 10% off your mortgage once a year, thus reducing the loan. Most property investors choose to have interest-only mortgages, thus never using their own money other than their first deposit.

Successful property investment is a long-term game, and it makes good business sense if you have money floating around, to invest in additional properties instead of paying chunks off your current mortgages.

If a property hasn't increased in value, there are lenders who allow 80% LTV (Loan to Value) products. The problem currently doesn't seem to be the house value increasing but the rental in order for the affordability calculator to work, but it is a possibility.

This is only a rough guide because we can't speak for individual lenders' criteria or how the current economic climate is by the time you read this book, which is why it is important to have a good financial advisor to advise you.

Other Options:

Of course, there are other options for getting a second deposit together as we mentioned at the beginning of the book; credit cards, personal loans, joint ventures etc. However, you already have an asset worth thousands of pounds just sitting there, available to pull money out – why wouldn't you use that to your advantage?

Successful property investors never use their own money! They cleverly use the assets they already own; they take calculated risks and use lenders to their advantage. Once you have one property, you create a snowball effect.

The Snowball Effect:

Property investment soon becomes a snowball effect when done correctly. By this, I mean, your ability to add to your portfolio increases much like a snowball – the more you add to it, the greater it grows.

When I purchased my first property, the money I had saved up and invested as the deposit meant that the value of the property was far greater than what I owed to my mortgage lender. And because I had bought it as less than market value, meant that it was worth more than what I originally paid for it. I was able to take 80% of the value of the property out which was enough to pay for three deposits on three new properties.

This is a system that I have used ever since. Every time I buy a property, I always try to buy it at less than the asking price, then in the future, when it's increased in value or my mortgage agreement is coming to an end, Jason will renegotiate a better lender and pull out any equity out of it.

Obviously doing this doesn't always come for nothing – lenders often charge a fee to renegotiate a mortgage, but you do usually have the option to add this to your new loan amount.

You also have to pay your financial advisor for their work

and of course stamp duty and solicitor's fees for every new purchase. Which is why it is important to make sure that the property that you are buying is going to be a good rental and will attract a good yield.

HMO's

HMO's are homes of multiple occupancy and are fast becoming a popular alternative for property investors and landlords.

A HMO is a single property that has been divided up into rooms for individual renters. Whilst it seems a no-brainer to be able to get much more rental income for a single property than just renting it out to a family, there are a lot more rules and regulations that you need to adhere to if you're thinking about becoming a HMO landlord.

To start with, mortgage lenders need to know that you are intending to run a HMO when you apply for a mortgage, or if you decide to change from a standard BTL mortgage. Your insurance company will also need to know because there is more of a risk to a property, the more people are living in it.

You will also have to apply to your local council for a HMO licence. Each council varies. Whilst the governmental website states the following:

If you want to rent out your property as a house in multiple occupation in England or Wales, you must contact your council to check if you need a licence.

You must have a licence if you're renting out a large HMO in England or Wales. Your property is defined as a large HMO if all of the following apply:

- It is rented to five or more people who are from more than one household
- Some or all tenants share a toilet, bathroom, or kitchen facilities

- At least one tenant pays rent (or their employer pays it for them)

You will still have to contact your local council to see what their definition of a HMO letting is. My local council states that a property is classed as a HMO where two or more people, not related to each other, are living in one property and as such, requires a HMO licence. A licence is valid for five years and will have to be renewed.

Your HMO licence will cost between £400 and £700, depending on your local council.

Conditions of a HMO

The very basic requirements of renting a HMO are:

- The house is suitable for the number of occupants (this depends on its size and facilities).
- The manager of the house – you or an agent – is considered to be 'fit and proper', for example they have no criminal record or breach of landlord laws or code of practice.
- The property has an updated gas safety certificate every year and an electrical check certificate every five years.
- You install and maintain smoke alarms/carbon monoxide detectors.
- You provide safety certificates for all electrical appliances when requested.
- You provide a fire extinguisher/fire blanket in the property.

Again, depending on your local council's requirements most insist on:

- All communal areas (hall, kitchen, bathrooms, communal lounges) are cleaned once a week.

- Fire doors are fitted in the kitchen.
- Every room has a means of fire escape.
- Every room has its own lock on the door.
- You have a communal noticeboard on display with contact information listed.
- Every resident receives a copy of their own rental contract.
- There is a copy of the gas safety certificate, HMO license, EPC and electrical certificate on the noticeboard.
- All rooms are required to have a smoke alarm installed and a carbon monoxide alarm if you have any gas in the property.
- There must be a means of entry and exit at the front of the property.
- If your property is on more than three floors, you must have a fire escape on the top floor.
- You are legally required to have one bathroom per every four tenants, but the more the better.
- You are legally required to have a communal dining room in your property.
- All HMO's must comply with fire-safety regulations and have a regular fire-safety check. Your local council will tell you how often this will be.

Tenants' Rooms:

You have to remember that every room in your HMO is someone's home and personal living space. Every room needs to be furnished with the basics – a bed, a wardrobe or some means of storage, lighting, a bed-side table, flooring and blinds or curtains.

Because many students rent HMO's, it's ideal to also include some shelving and a desk and chair. These days, most people own a computer and a phone, so it's a good idea to fit sockets with USB ports included. They cost a few pounds more than standard sockets, but your tenants will thank you for including them.

Another good idea is to include a safe in each tenant's room. This provides them with a bit of security in their own room. Some landlords also include a portable TV in each room, but these are not requirements.

Single bedrooms need to be a minimum of 6.5 square metres and doubles are a minimum of 8 square metres.

Kitchen:

The kitchen needs to be designed as a working kitchen, so you have to provide everything that you would find in any other kitchen. This includes cutlery for the number of tenants living there, utensils, a microwave, washing-up bowl, cooker, fridge/ freezer, and an eating area large enough for the number of tenants you have.

Most kitchen designs come with an integrated dishwasher, but this isn't a legal requirement if yours doesn't have one.

There needs to be enough storage cupboards for each tenant to have their own if they wish.

A smoke alarm and carbon monoxide alarm must be fitted in the kitchen area, along with a fire extinguisher and fire blanket.

Dining Room:

You can have a dining area within the kitchen, but it's better if you can designate a separate room as a dining room. Your dining room needs a table and enough chairs for the number of tenants living in the property.

Communal Lounge:

Every HMO property needs to have a communal lounge which needs to be a minimum of 10 square metres.

Your lounge should have a large TV, enough seating for the number of tenants in the property, lighting, such as lamps, and flooring. Due to the amount of wear and tear that occurs in a HMO, it's better to cover your floors with hardwood and washable rugs, rather than carpet. A book shelf and coffee table are ideal to put in the lounge. Furniture doesn't have to be new; you can pick up a lot of second-hand furniture that will be suitable for a HMO. As long as it's all clean and functional.

Hallway:

Your hallway must be free of clutter. If tenants own bicycles, they need to be stored in a shed outside or in their own rooms. A clear hallway is necessary in case there's a fire in the house and the tenant's need to escape the building.

Utilities:

When you rent a property to a family or a single tenant, they are usually always responsible for their utility bills, council tax, etc. When you rent a HMO you usually include the cost of all utilities in the rent. This will include gas, electric, water, council tax (although if it's student accommodation they will be exempt from this), and should you wish to include it, internet use.

Not every HMO provides internet usage, but if you're letting to students, they will expect it.

Different HMO landlords have different ways of working out the utility usage for their tenants. Some work out an average use and add this to the tenant's monthly rent, others divide their quarterly bill between the number of tenants and ask them to pay it every quarter.

To prevent a tenant from exploiting the use of water and heating, many landlords will fit a timer meter in a locked cupboard so that the heating and hot water will be available two times a day. Other landlords control their heating and hot water by an app on their phone. I personally think this is a bit mean and utilities should be freely available at any time of the day or night, but some landlords have found that it can get abused and their tenants leave the heating on in the middle of summer.

Nevertheless it's important that you work the average costs into your rental charge from the beginning.

Additional Info:

Because a HMO generally houses people that do not know each other, as a landlord you need to be prepared that arguments can break out and your role of landlord will often include mediator and peacekeeper. There are very few letting agents prepared to manage HMOs because it's a lot more work than a single let.

Tenants of HMOs have the same legal tenancy rights as any other tenant, but you usually find that you will have a higher turnover of them because tenants of HMOs are often students or people needing a short-term place to live.

As with a normal tenancy agreement, each tenant will be contracted for a minimum of six months, but some landlords are happy to draw up an agreement on a per term/per college year basis.

The Figures:

Let's look at an example of the rental potential for a five-bed, terrace house in town. I'm estimating figures based on the south-west area where I live, but these could differ from town to town.

Basic rental potential if rented to a family:

Based on the current rents, a five-bed property in my town would fetch around **£1,200 PCM**.

Supposing your mortgage on the property costs **£250 PCM**.

This gives you a profit of **£950 PCM**, before maintenance costs are deducted.

Rental potential if run as a HMO:

Based on the current rates for a single room in my area, you could ask for a minimum of **£450 PCM**

Multiply this by five occupants - **£2,250 PCM**

Mortgage costs - **£250 PCM**

Average utility, cleaning, and insurance costs - **£150 PCM**

This gives you a profit of **£1,850 PCM**, before maintenance costs are deducted.

As you can see, you have almost doubled your profit on exactly the same property.

The Advantages and Disadvantages of HMOs:
Advantages:

The pros of owning a HMO are as follows:

- You can easily make a lot more money than if you rented your property to one person/family.
- Rents are usually paid direct to you from either the council or college/university.
- You will never be short of tenants.
- Despite having several tenants, you only have one property to maintain.

Disadvantages:

- You have to make sure you are compliant with your council's and legal HMO requirements.
- You could have to deal with more disputes than if you just rented your property to one person/one family.
- You have to make sure that all communal areas are safe and clean every week.
- You may have gap rental periods between tenants – i.e. when students leave college or tenants move on.

AirBnB and Holiday Lets:

AirBnB is one of the most popular choices for holiday makers who prefer to stay in a home, rather than a hotel and is a viable option for a property investor.

If you have a property that is located close to the seaside, an area of natural beauty or even close to a vibrant city, then using your property as an AirBnB is an ideal option. You can earn a lot more in holiday lets than privately renting.

Most property investors don't buy a property with the intention of letting it out as a holiday home. If you do, you will need to notify your mortgage lender and change your mortgage to a holiday-let mortgage. Until a few years ago, many lenders were opposed to holiday-let mortgages, but they have had to learn to accommodate their customers.

Today, most lenders are happy to switch your mortgage over – and back again if you decide holiday lets are not for you.

It's not just holiday makers that use AirBnB either. A lot of business people need somewhere to stay during the working week, so if you have a property that is in the city and near a train station, you are in a prime location to offer your services.

The advantages and disadvantages of Holiday Lets:

Advantages:

- You can charge a day or week rate, meaning that your income can be substantially higher than any other rental opportunity.
- If your property is in a good location, you will never be short of house guests.
- If you join up with Airbnb, all admin and finance is provided for you.
- You have the opportunity to meet lots of new people.

Disadvantages:

- You may have weeks without any guests booked in, but you will still have to cover the mortgage.
- You have to furnish your holiday let and provide everything you would find in a typical home, including

bed linen, towels, and kitchen equipment.

- Unless you hire someone, you will be responsible for cleaning the property between guests.
- You will need to be on hand to welcome guests and provide a contact in case they need you during their stay.

Homeless Prevention Scheme:

I first came across the council's Homeless Prevention Scheme a few years ago when another investor mentioned it to me and it is something I am extremely passionate about.

According to Shelter's latest figures, there are 280,000 people in England who are registered as homeless and there are thousands more at risk of losing their home than ever before.

The Homelessness Reduction Act came into force in April 2017 and enforces every local council to take responsibility for homeless people in their area.

Due to the lack of affordable social housing, councils have enlisted the help of private property investors and landlords to persuade them to allow their properties to be rented by people and families who would otherwise be homeless.

I joined my council's scheme in 2019 and five of my properties are rented out to them to provide a safe and secure home for some of their clients who were registered as homeless.

There's a huge misconception about homeless people and I wish the councils would change the title of their schemes. Most people think of the homeless as people you see on every high street up and down the country, begging for money. Unfortunately, these are just the people you see. You don't see the families who, through no fault of their own, are made homeless. The reasons can vary; from a landlord increasing their rent to an amount that they can no longer afford, to a family break-up resulting in one partner moving out, a death of a family member or a landlord having to sell their home.

I've spoken to a lot of landlords and encouraged them to

look past the word 'homeless' and realise that homelessness is usually down to a person's circumstances and that it can affect anyone at any time in their life.

How to join the Homeless Prevention Scheme:

Your local council should have a scheme in place. Although it might be called something slightly different, it will still deal with helping people who might be faced with the prospect of becoming homeless.

My local team assess a property to make sure it's suitable and up to letting standards. If a property requires some work, they pay towards the costs prior to a tenant being offered it. My council also offer a 'thank you' payment to every landlord by way of thanks for allowing the council to let your property, but again, this may differ from area to area.

Deposits, references, and checks:

The council hold a deposit in the form of a bond for every landlord in case a tenant causes any damage to your property. They usually have a list of prospective tenants already looking for a permanent home, who will have already been thoroughly vetted and referenced and will work through the list to see who might be most suitable and most in need of being offered a home.

I've found that my local team are strict in who they put forward as potential tenants and I had the opportunity to meet all the applicants and answer any questions they might have.

Tenancies:

As with any other tenancy, your contract will be between you and your tenant, not the council. My area insist on a 12 month AST so that it provides a bit of security for the tenant and they also offer a rent guarantee scheme so that you will always receive your rent on time, even if a tenant falls behind.

Advantages and disadvantages of the Homeless Scheme:

Advantages:

- You will always have a tenant in your property.
- Your rent is guaranteed.
- You are helping people in need.
- The council act as your agent.
- You don't pay any commission.
- The council carry out regular inspections on your behalf for nothing.

Disadvantages:

- You usually have to sign a minimum 12-month contract.
- Most councils don't deal with maintenance or repairs – you will be responsible for these.

Buying a Property Abroad:

Given that properties abroad are often a lot cheaper than in the UK, it's very tempting to consider this as a viable option, not only as a holiday home for yourself, but to be able to rent it out the times you're not using it. What could be more appealing than to have somewhere to holiday, but also make money from it?

Although I've considered buying property abroad, it's not something I have personal experience of yet. However, despite leaving the EU there are still options to buying abroad, but you need to keep yourself updated with any changes that the Foreign and Commonwealth office implement.

If this is something you like the idea of, it's important to find an agent that specialises in buying property abroad. Right Move have a wealth of information on their website at https://www.rightmove.co.uk/overseas-property/help-and-advice/research.html which will guide you through the whole process.

Each country will have its own legislation regarding purchasing a property as an international buyer and their taxes, agent fees, etc., will be very different to the ones we're used to in the UK.

Whilst you will see that many properties abroad are a fraction of the price than in the UK, there may be different regulations and costs in the country you are hoping to buy a property in, so always get expert advice before committing to buying a property abroad.

Many UK lenders have the option to offer overseas mortgages, but again this is a specialist area of conveyancing and not every lender will be qualified to deal with this type of mortgage.

It is highly advisable to use a firm that specialises in currency transfers when you come to send money abroad for buying a property. Specialist currency companies offer better exchange rates than most banks for foreign currency transfers. They also have clever ways of protecting your money from fluctuating exchange rates between the point of agreeing to buy property abroad and completing on it – during which time, the price in Sterling can vary dramatically.

www.aplaceinthesun.com/advice/lettings is an excellent source to buying property abroad as a rental.

The advantages of investing abroad:

- You get more property for your money and a property often comes with land which you can build on.
- You have a ready-made holiday home.
- You will always be able to let your property out, particularly if it's in a popular destination.
- Maintenance and building costs are generally cheaper than in the UK.

The disadvantages of investing abroad:

- You need to thoroughly research the legalities of the

country you are planning to buy in.

- The language barrier can be a problem unless you are fluent in their language.
- A property abroad might be a quarter of the price in the UK but consider if there are any additional taxes/fees to pay.
- Because there is more risk to buying an overseas property, your initial deposit might be higher than a UK BTL.
- You will not be on call should anything go wrong with your property, so you will have to hire someone local to the area to manage your property.

It's very important to find an estate agent and solicitor that specialises in overseas property buying when considering this as an option.

There are many other options for you to earn money from property, such as B&B, halfway houses, hostels, student housing, etc.

Flipping:

Property investors tend to fall into one of two camps; they either decide to rent their properties out or they buy a property to do up and sell – known as flipping.

Flipping is an ideal option if you want to turn a profit quickly and can be combined successfully with running a rental business. If you can find a cheap property, perhaps at auction, and can add value to it, you stand to make a good profit by flipping it, giving you access to a large amount of cash to reinvest in another property. I did this with the first house I bought at auction.

Some property investors prefer to flip their properties rather than deal with running a rental business and this is a good idea if you don't want the headache of dealing with tenants and all the landlord legalities that go with renting a property. However, you can only ever flip a property once. You will forever be able to rent a property out.

It's all a matter of preference and I know several property investors who do a combination of both buying to rent and buying to flip.

SHOULD YOU START A LIMITED COMPANY?

Most first-time property investors start with a single property bought in their own name or that of them and their partner. As I mentioned before, most property investors soon discover just how easy it is to use that initial property as a means to buy another property and so on.

Many lenders have a cap on the amount of properties they will lend you on. For some they will allow up to six per person, others will allow up to 10. If you have a spouse, some lenders will consider lending 10 to each person, or allow you to purchase more in joint names.

In addition to this, if you have children over the age of 21, some lenders will allow you to apply as a joint applicant with your child, but it does all depend on the lender's criteria – again this is another good reason to have a good financial advisor who will know the different lenders' application criteria.

At some point, if you decide you want to expand your portfolio, you will exhaust your individual criteria for lending, and you may have to consider other options such as starting a limited company.

There is no one-size-fits-all answer to whether you should start a limited company or continue to trade as a sole-trader with your property business. It really is a case of getting good accounting and tax advice from a professional who specialises in limited companies.

The advantages of setting up a limited company:
- There may be better tax breaks on having a limited

company, particularly if you intend to grow your portfolio.

- If you have a second income and don't need to rely on the income from your properties you can reinvest in more properties and you won't pay income tax on your rental income – although you will be responsible for paying corporation tax.
- It is easier to transfer ownership of a property owned by a limited company by way of a share transfer.
- There is no tax on dividends of up to £5,000, meaning you can draw this amount out of your business without having to pay tax on it.
- It is often easier to use your limited company again and again once a mortgage lender accepts you.

The disadvantages of setting up a limited company:

- There are fewer lenders available to borrow from and interest rates are usually higher.
- If you have other shareholders in your company, you will not own 100% of the shares and will require a shareholder agreement for protection.
- Should you sell a property in your limited company, you will be required to pay corporation tax on the profits.
- You will need to keep accurate records, including paying yourself a salary/dividends from your company to yourself.
- The length of conveyancing time it takes for a sale to go through can take longer.
- There is no personal Capital Gains Tax allowance if you sell a property.
- If you wish to transfer existing properties to your limited company, you will have to pay Stamp Duty – most accountants advise to leave your individual properties where they are.

As you can see, there are many advantages and disadvantages to setting up a limited company and it's vital that you get professional advice because each case will be different depending on how much you want to expand your business.

If you decide to start a limited company you will have to apply and register with Companies House (https://www.gov.uk/set-up-limited-company)

You will also be required to open a separate bank account in your company name. Even if you don't use your limited company for a while, you will still need to submit your accounts to the tax office yearly, but you can have your limited company classed as 'dormant' until you decide you wish to use it for your business.

PROPERTY SCAMS:

Because property investment is one of the safest and most reliable areas of achieving a passive income, there is also an ever-increasing platform for scams in this industry.

From YouTube videos promising how you can make millions in property with no outlay to free property seminars run all over the country, making the same promises that you will never have to work again; they're all out there.

I recently attended one such seminar which was being promoted in the name of a well-known property investor. Their name was plastered all over the literature, giving people the impression that this person would be attending and promising that by the end of the evening, you would be well on your way to becoming a multi-millionaire property investor.

The reality of it was that the well-known property investor didn't attend any of the seminars and it appeared that they were just lending their name to it.

The seminar was run by a young woman who kept telling the audience how stupid they were to have not already jumped on the property bandwagon. One hundred and fifty of us sat there being berated by a woman in a suit.

The seminar went on for a couple of hours, until the moment when she revealed just how we could all make our dreams of giving up the nine-to-five come true and never have to work again – for a fee.

The fee was over £1,000 to enrol on a property investment course, written by said well-known-person and worked out less than if you purchased 400 cups of coffee (or some such rubbish).

Two of the 150 participants signed up for more information on the 'for-one-night-only' offer, and I'm not sure if they were planted in the audience or not, but I abhor these sort of get-rich-quick tactics.

You may be wondering why I attended in the first place. Because I'm terribly nosy and I wanted to research how companies like this try to sell the dream to people. You could argue that by writing this book, I am profiting from selling the dream of being a property investor to other people. However, I would counterclaim this argument because I am simply passing on the information I have learned along the way, including all the mistakes I've made and the tips I've picked up and the easiest way for me to do that is to produce a book about it.

I have never once promised that you will get rich quickly or that it will be easy. It's a long-term career and you will have many ups and downs. Plus, I have tried to point out where I've made mistakes that have cost me thousands of pounds, so that you won't have to.

I agree that if you have a skill that can be passed on to others, you should be able to charge for it. What I don't agree with is the way some people charge ridiculous amounts of money, promising results that will never happen. I'm also very suspicious of people who have the time to run property seminars. If they are so successful, surely they don't need to travel up and down the country 'selling the dream'? You don't see Bill Gates hiring a hotel conference room and selling courses on how to become a billionaire, or Al Pacino running workshops on how to become an award-winning actor.

These seminars and conferences are similar to American evangelism churches. They stir people up with the belief that if only they believe, they will achieve. In reality, you will be parting with your hard-earned money for a course or an e-book that won't actually deliver what's been promised.

I can't reiterate enough that whilst investing in property can be very profitable, there is no quick way in to becoming a millionaire and any course, webinar or Facebook advert telling you otherwise is a ploy to get you to part with your cash and make the organisers richer.

Be careful of the adverts that are cropping up telling you that you can become a property investor with absolutely zero monetary investment. This is just not possible.

No one is going to hand over the keys to their property to you and allow you to rent it out for nothing. As we have seen at the beginning of the book, regardless of how you do it, you need to generate a deposit and you need to persuade a lender to lend the rest of the money to you to purchase a property. Nothing is given to you on a plate, so please don't fall for any promises like this.

How to Avoid Scams:

As tempting as it is to believe the promises of zero-risk property investment schemes, you are better off talking to other people who have already made a business out of investing in property.

It's taken me over seven years to learn what I know and most of it has been through trial and error and talking to other investors who themselves have learned lessons over the years. And I'm still learning.

Laws relating to landlords, tax issues, building regulations and property investment change all the time and it's important to keep up to date with the latest information. It also pays to belong to a landlords' forum because there will certainly be other landlords out there who are only too happy to share their own experiences, tips, and advice. We're not in competition with each other and are more than happy to pass on the information we've learned on our own journey.

I am very lucky and the majority of time that I've taken a calculated risk it has worked in my favour. Ironically, I never harboured dreams of being a landlord or a property investor, but it just kind of snowballed.

I've had my fair share of disasters on this journey into property investment. I've been ripped over for hundreds of thousands of pounds from people who I naively trusted. I've had tenants refuse to pay their rent for months. I've received death threats from tenants. I've been blackmailed and had a contractor try to run me over in the street and I've been called out in the middle of the night several times to attend to a property problem. Those are the times when I've wanted to throw the towel in, sell everything and move to Hawaii.

I've equally had some amazing times: the look of joy on a tenant's face when I hand over the keys to a permanent new home they've waited so long for, negotiating the price of a property and winning, being able to afford to help my friends and family out financially, making lifelong friends in the industry and learning new skills every day. I now feel qualified enough to write this book and pass my experience on to you, in the hope that you also take what you've learned from this to create your own property empire and make your own dreams of becoming financially independent come true.

If I could only give you one piece of advice it would be to start, regardless of your age – although I wish I had started investing when I was much younger. If you don't plan your own future, you'll always be where you are right now. It takes just one snowflake to create a snowball.

I hope that you have found this book helpful and wish you every success in your venture!

Deborah

15 Ways to Own Your Future
Take Control of Your Destiny in Business and in Life
Michael Khouri
A 15-point blueprint for creating better collaboration, enjoyment,
and success in business and in life.
Paperback: 978-1-78535-300-0 ebook: 978-1-78535-301-7

The Common Excuses of the Comfortable Compromiser
Understanding Why People Oppose Your Great Idea
Matt Crossman
Comfortable compromisers block the way of anyone trying to
change anything. This is your guide to their common excuses.
Paperback: 978-1-78099-595-3 ebook: 978-1-78099-596-0

The Failing Logic of Money
Duane Mullin
Money is wasteful and cruel, causes war, crime and dysfunctional
feudalism. Humankind needs happiness, peace and abundance. So
banish money and use technology and knowledge to rid the world
of war, crime and poverty.
Paperback: 978-1-84694-259-4 ebook: 978-1-84694-888-6

Mastering the Mommy Track
Juggling Career and Kids in Uncertain Times
Erin Flynn Jay
Mastering the Mommy Track tells the stories of everyday working
mothers, the challenges they have faced, and lessons learned.
Paperback: 978-1-78099-123-8 ebook: 978-1-78099-124-5

Modern Day Selling

Unlocking Your Hidden Potential
Brian Barfield
Learn how to reconnect sales associates with customers and unlock hidden sales potential.
Paperback: 978-1-78099-457-4 ebook: 978-1-78099-458-1

The Most Creative, Escape the Ordinary, Excel at Public Speaking Book Ever

All The Help You Will Ever Need in Giving a Speech
Philip Theibert
The 'everything you need to give an outstanding speech' book, complete with original material written by a professional speech-writer.
Paperback: 978-1-78099-672-1 ebook: 978-1-78099-673-8

Readers of ebooks can buy or view any of these bestsellers by clicking on the live link in the title. Most titles are published in paperback and as an ebook. Paperbacks are available in traditional bookshops. Both print and ebook formats are available online.
Find more titles and sign up to our readers' newsletter at
http://www.jhpbusiness-books.com/
Facebook: https://www.facebook.com/JHPNonFiction/
Twitter: @JHPNonFiction